ANGEL DEVONE

breathe again

How to protect your heart, realize your power and regain control of your life through self-discovery.

Ms Lisa
as you turn the
pages I pray tha[...]
anything broken or mi[...]
will be restored.
thanks for your support
Love
Angel
2019

Breathe Again: How to Protect Your Heart, Realize Your Power and Regain Control of Your Life Through Self-Discovery
by Angel Devone

www.angelpdevone.com
info@angelpdevone.com

Cover Design by PDG Branding & Marketing

Edited by:
Tiffany Buckner
Stephanie Anderson

Interior Design: Anointed Fire House

ISBN-13: 978-0-692-05104-7

I have tried to recreate events, locales and conversations from my memories of them. In order to maintain their anonymity in some instances I have changed the names of individuals and places, I may have changed some identifying characteristics and details such as physical properties, occupations and places of residence.

Dedication and Acknowledgments

I dedicate this book to my grandmother, Lucy P. Murray. The first black Miss Savannah of 1948, Lucy P. Murray is a true legend. She always fought to beat her last best record, never settling for just ordinary. She literally broke barriers in her generation during her lifetime. At age 60 (after retirement) she graduated magna cum laude from Savannah State University with a degree in Social Work. She did not allow her age to impede her goals. Because of Lucy P. Murray, I understand just why my head should be held high. I can't even begin to talk about the grace of her style. Even at the age of 84, she had aspirations of continuing her career as a seamstress. She often told me to shoot for the stars because, as she said, I can have anything that I want. Nana, I apologize for not finishing this book while you were alive to read it. You are a phenomenal woman and your sacrifices, along with your legacy, will never be forgotten. It is with honor and joy that I dedicate my book "Breathe Again" to you!! LUCY P. MURRAY 1932-2016.

To my mother, Angela Lockwood, my maternal grandmother, Mae Lockwood, and my Aunt Denise Henderson: Thank you for being my backbone while I was going through life and while I was writing this book. I could not have done this without you.

To my entire family: You all have supported me since day one. For you, I am grateful.

This book is also dedicated to all people, but especially to women. To every woman who has forgotten to love themselves while trying to love others. To every woman who has been secretly depressed, but still working to be a contributing member of the society. To all of my sisters who have hidden in the shadows of greatness, knowing that you have an innate craving to offer your perspective and expertise. To those who feel guilty about your success and for being favored by God. Even to those who have faked like they had it all, but deep within wanted to be genuinely fulfilled. It's to you that I have written this book. Women are the heartbeat of this society and the thread that holds families together, but sometimes knowing this truth has been to the detriment of our own self-care. Just as much as you are willing to care for others, you deserve to take even better care for yourselves. As you intentionally care for yourself completely, not excluding your psychological health, you have the power to improve every aspect of your life. Every part of your existence that died has the ability to be resurrected and revived.

Lastly, to those who have never paid a bill late. You have always had it together, you know who you are perfectly well, you were born into the perfect family, your spices are in alphabetical order in your cabinet and you have never had to cry yourself to sleep. You love everyone, even yourself perfectly. You're never insecure. Your kids are perfect. You have never lied, hurt anyone or stabbed anyone in the back. All of your friends think you got it all together. This book is also for you. My prayer is that your heart will be opened to receive all of God's love for you so that you can embrace your true self— this is the you who is far from perfect. I pray that you become all that you were created to be. I'm committed to taking the journey with you because I am you. We are in this together.

With Love,
Angel

TABLE OF CONTENTS

INTRODUCTION

To understand the phenomenon of breathing again from my reality, this book pulls together years of adversity that led to a journey of recovery. It combines years of insight that I gained from taking the steps to pull myself out of a place of stifled purpose. But, I also reveal the painful experience that I brought on myself due to lack of self-discovery. My goal is to help those who read this book to locate themselves and use the tools that I have provided, coupled with their inner power, to reach their desired quality of life. I will reveal exactly what I did to become a woman who is self-aware and not identified by societal standards—standards that are contrary to God's standards. This book marries my research, insight, personal experiences and some thoughts of the people who contributed to my life's transformation.

During this journey, you will discover your purpose and become aware of what you want. I will extensively highlight the various dimensions of God and how we gain our identities from who He is and what He says about us. You will learn how to answer the questions:

1. What can I live without?
2. Who am I?
3. What is my purpose?
4. What do I want?

These are all questions that reveal your identity and show that you are aware of who you are. Not only that, you will be able to use your discovery to create something great that this generation as well as future generations can benefit from. The answers to these questions will help you to create a vision for your life, kick the need for approval to the curb, foster compassion for yourself, stop comparing yourself to others, reprogram your thinking and live your best life in real life. You will also learn my framework for facilitating the process. This includes what I like to call, breathing techniques that will empower you to take an active role in your development and empowerment.

I will expose the myths or lies that we have heard — distortions that we have allowed to shape our lives. You will know how to identify the tactics that the enemy uses to keep you mediocre and prohibit you from fully realizing your power. By the end of this book, you will never again use your job, a failure, bank account, relationships or material possessions to define who you are, and you will not allow others to control your life. You will not dim your light in a world that is waiting on you to shine. You will know what it takes to have full control of your life. You will be armed with the biblical knowledge that has practical application. The information shared here will help you make decisions that positively affect your well-being; that is, assuming that you bring your full attention, intention and discipline to practicing these self-discovery steps.

You're about to enter a very transformational period that will take you to the point of exceeding your last best self, even if these changes first manifest in your mind before you see them in your life. I'm less concerned about you having the house, car and mate that you want. Although you deserve it, if you can't think well of yourself without these things, you will not be able to sustain your earnings.

WHY NOW? WHY THIS BOOK?

I'm a very compassionate woman. My compassion genuinely comes from being able to see myself in every woman that I talk to. I am every woman! To add to this, there is an unrelenting war that life wages against our identities every day. With the media telling us how we should look, dress, date, dream and live, we have a lot to overcome. Not to mention, there are people who want to take credit for the few accomplishments that we have made. We obligate ourselves to tasks we don't want and we overextend ourselves to be liked. Some of us even hide our gifts to be liked. This is enough to exhaust anyone. For some, there is a sense that they will never be able to rise above the past trauma, failures or the current distractions. On the other side, what I have seen is that more and more women are ready to make a change.

Of course, you may be living a happy life, all the while wondering if it will all come tumbling down. "How do I sustain this happiness?" you might ask. You may be tired of the troughs that sometimes come with life. Good thing, troughs do not take away happiness. I get it. You don't want any more tricks, nursery rhymes or old wives' tales that will merely change your mood. You need systems and mental shifts that will help you to form habits for maintaining and advancing your life.

Though everyone has a way of sometimes hiding what bothers, weakens or sets them back, they all want to advance. I can attest to the fact that hiding and denying negative emotions will cause collateral damage, like ruined relationships, financial ruin, insecurity, loss of social dignity, uncontrolled stress and mental dysfunction. We have all worried about such things at some point, but the fact that it has been accomplished before makes the odds of accomplishing it again even greater. Hence the title, Breathe AGAIN.

You are more than able to become better, but what warrants better behavior is self-discovery. You may find that you are better at some things than others, for example, you may have uncharted confidence in your ability to be a good employer or a good wife, but your confidence wanes in your ability to make good decisions without considering the opinions of others. Your professional skills may be unmatched, but you hate yourself at the end of the day if you make a mistake or if you don't feel perfect. You can motivate yourself and keep yourself inspired, but sometimes, your flaws and fears speak louder than your inspiration. You've seen some of your friends or people you don't know just glide with grace through life, succeeding in every endeavor, no matter what comes their way. Nothing threatens their uniqueness because they know their power and what they have to offer, and they use these strengths for their benefit. Do they have a secret that they are not telling the rest of us? NO. They know who they are and how to use it to their benefit. They have a vision for their lives and they make decisions that are in alignment with their vision. They have accepted that they are not perfect, and are now allowing their lives to be guided by their discovered purpose and the Giver of that purpose. The amazing news is that you were created with the same breath that is infusing them to win and be successful. It all starts with discovering YOURSELF!

My Search for ME

One may say that a few (if any) great literary works are created suddenly. The ideas they contain, the blood, sweat, fears and even the sacrifices made to execute the ideas, almost invariably emanate from years of experience, misfortune and/or dedication to a subject of study to the point of mastery. When I first started to write this book, I had already lived some of the experiences that would someday fill the pages of this book. But the one thing that would legitimize the experiences and bind the book together would be my intentional pursuit and procurement of the gift of healing and restoration, which had not taken place. Not to mention, I didn't even know how to articulate the insight that I'd gained from my experiences to write a book.

In 2013, when I started jotting my ideas on a legal tablet, I was broken from the experiences of my past and unable to live a quality lifestyle consistently. I was not spiritually sound, nor was I mentally or emotionally stable. Seriously! My heart was broken from toxic relationships. I was wounded from the rejection, bruised by the emotional turmoil caused by molestation, tormented by incessant thoughts of hopelessness and troubled by the anxiety of it all. Wretched, or as we say today, RATCHET was an understatement to describe who I had become. My life had no semblance of peace. I was good for no-ONE and no-THING, not even myself. Life was dark and I was full of ignorance concerning my identity and purpose. Surprisingly enough, I still managed to achieve limited amounts of success. However, I continued harboring resentment and anger from past hurts, rejections and failures, so much so that even the success that I did achieve felt like a curse. To outsiders looking into my world, it may have looked like all was well, and that's because people don't get a chance to experience me the same way that I experience me, plus, I knew how to fake it. I really wanted to be well, but I just wasn't. You know how we do as women — we know how to make everyone think that we are living the good life when, in reality, we are not even living. For some reason, I bought into the idea that it's okay to "fake it until you make it." I was good at it.

I knew that God had given me a story that I would one day be able to share with the world. Perhaps, the time that I started to write the book was just not advantageous enough to produce hearty content because I had not addressed my pain. After all, I had gone through the hurt, but no healing had taken place. I thought, "How in the world do I venture to help someone heal when I myself have unhealed wounds?" I had not even forgiven those who'd hurt me, nor had I forgiven myself. I had not settled, and because of this, I saw myself turning into the people who hurt me. I had always heard the old adage that said, "Hurt people, hurt people." The greater truth is that hurt people continue to hurt themselves. There is no way to love others if we hate ourselves. We try it, but what we offer is a dangerous type of love. I did not want to be like that! I honestly did not wish the feelings that I was having or the mental state that I was in on my worst enemy.

I was wounded. A wounded heart can't be productive or effective on a consistent basis. My goal. as a person. was to be healed so that I could use my story to facilitate the process of healing to others. While I believe that being broken makes us more relatable and able to share with others, I wanted and needed to be mended first.

While I believe that, at some point, we should all endeavor in life to help others along the way, we should not feel guilty for wanting to exercise self-care first. I have become a student of the Bible. In it, God commands us to love our neighbor as ourselves. So, it behooves us to be in a place where we can share the love that we were commanded to share.

In my opinion, service would be more effective in the event that those serving obtain counsel for personal issues and have cleared the residue of a mentality birthed in adversity. I am sure you have heard Matthew 15:14 being quoted. In summary, it says, "If the blind tries to lead the blind, they will both fall into a ditch." Granted, no one is perfect, this scripture implicitly suggests that if one's vision is blurred or his or her outlook has been tainted, something needs to be done to bring clarity to that person's vision before it's okay for that person to lead. This is simply because when a person is mentally and emotionally unstable, that person will focus on his or her pain, rather than focusing on the problem itself.

I do believe that individuals who may be experiencing resistance in an area can indeed help others heal IF and only IF the necessary steps have been taken to, at least, identify and grasp control of the "issue" that troubles them. Let me explain. With a grateful heart, I can publicly express that I no longer suffer from clinical depression and anxiety. With God's guidance, I took the intentional steps to eventually cure myself of the disorder (you will learn my exact steps in a later chapter). However, by no means does this healing suggest that the feelings of depression and anxiety do not try to rear their ugly head or that I don't "feel" despondent some days. The truth is that I do. It would be irresponsible of me to try to convince you to believe that I have not experienced depression. Since I have been healed, I now understand and interpret healing to be something that one must know, rather than it being a feeling.

The difference between now and then is this: back then, depression dominated my existence. I was entangled by its sneaky symptoms: loss of appetite, shortness of breath, loss of interest, memory loss, and thoughts of hopelessness. The symptoms were the deceptive implications and the behaviors that supported the lies I believed about myself. and they were the result of misplaced purpose. I let it possess my life, steal my joy and manage my cognition. Nowadays, I have developed control over it. Actually, by structuring my daily routine and through relentless prayer, meditation, professional counseling, questioning God, self-examination and learning that my identity is in Christ, I have beat my enemy at his own game. Do I have it all together? No! And my spices are not in alphabetical order in my cabinet. I'm also not infallible. I have honestly learned to embrace my weaknesses. My weaknesses remind me that I can't do anything aside from God.

Furthermore, even in the face of adversity, I understand that a life without challenges would reduce all possibilities of personal growth down to none. So, on the days that I wake up and that nasty feeling shows up, I know how to push through it. I now know how to command that my day aligns with God's Word. The one way I learned to fight emotional and mental obstacles is through intentional practices. No longer do I accept depression as my normal.

Some days, I don't feel ready to take that next step or even advance to the next level. But waiting to feel ready may never come. I may feel intimidated and inadequate, but that's why I've become intentionally SELF-motivated. And I have realized that sometimes, I feel inadequate only because this whole idea that I can do something that no one else can do is so CRAZY that I can't wrap my mind around it. I am up for the challenge, nonetheless. I'm finally committed to being successful at the thing that makes my existence necessary. One thing about life is that success is not going to come without pressure. The first level of pressure is defining who you are and what success means to you without the influence of other mediums outside of YOU.

It's time to put your uniqueness on display for the world to see. This is what makes you REAL. Many people think that being real is about giving someone a piece of their minds. So, they make someone feel bad and then justify their actions by saying, "I'm just being real." REAL has become such a catch-phrase that its organic meaning has been so far removed from the motivation behind the word. Well, I want to bring context to or re-brand, if you will, what REAL means.

When I first began to search for my identity, I looked to my career, fitness, Facebook likes, my connections, my Delta frequent flyer miles, my closet and my degree, among other things. I mean, I searched high and low. Eventually, I made my way to Jesus, and He was there to welcome me with open arms. He took me to a sequence of scriptures, and within the scriptures, the characteristics of who He says that we are spelled out the word REAL. He then whispered to me, "This is who you are. You are Righteous, you are

Esteemed, you are Accepted and you are Loved." In that moment, I felt the love of Jesus so tangibly that tears began to pour down my face. I knew then that nothing, not even my past or my present, my imperfections or my frailties, what people said or didn't say — NO-THING could compete against who God made me to be. He gave me this because of His love for me. You are REAL.

I have the pleasure of speaking with different women — many of them have said to me:

1. "I'm not confident that I'm on the right path."
2. "I've gotten into some trouble that I can't recover from."
3. "I don't go after what I want because I fear failure and rejection, or I compare myself to people who have the same occupation."

I usually say to them, "Everything you need to win is already inside of you. You came to this world with a gift that we are waiting on you to share. You just have to discover it. You have to discover the REAL you. This is the you who is like nothing that you have ever seen or experienced before. And your gift makes you necessary. Once you get the revelation, no one can take it from you. Your gift includes a solution for your problem and the fuel you'll need for your own progression." I've been able to understand these questions because I've asked the same questions and had the same concerns.

I have found the Bible to be a book about self-awareness and identity in Christ, so throughout this book, you will find several biblical references. I find the teachings in it about self-confidence, creating boundaries, courage, hope, personal development, mental health, individuality, love, forgiveness, self-esteem and other characteristics of our identities. I am excited that you have given me the distinct honor of being your guide as I endeavor to take you on a journey. I will challenge you to live according to what God says about you. I wrote this book because I need you to breathe, knowing you are Righteous, Esteemed, Accepted and Loved.

This book may not provide any quick-fix solutions and maybe no absolute answers, but it does provide supplementary approaches of how to overcome identity concerns. The idea to keep at the forefront of your mind is that identity is an element of life that is as essential as the air we breathe. This is because identity does to the soul what breathing does to the body. Identity is the breath of the soul. I promise that this will make more sense as you turn the pages. As you read on, please consider God's leadings and promptings as they will be the keys to total freedom

IDENTITY DISCOVERY LESSONS

This book is the fulcrum of my commitment to strengthen my sisters using my very own experiences. I have vowed to never seek information that I'm not willing to share, or hide solutions to problems that will help others become empowered. My work and research into self-discovery have allowed me to speak in prisons, churches, community events and schools. Most of all, it allows me to impact lives from a place of having done the work myself. My prayer is that one day, this work will allow me to build an empire and a legacy that won't be erased from history. This book not only spans years of my own personal development, but it includes data from some previously developed and proven systems — studies of concepts that predate my personally designed system.

HOW TO MAKE THE MOST OF THIS BOOK

You bought this book for one of several reasons. You are ready to Breathe Again-protect your heart, realize your power and take control of your life. I am going to show you how to execute each using my five breathing techniques. Maybe you want to support my endeavors to agitate how we have been programmed to think. Either reason is great. Both require action. But, there are risks involved, with one of them being that your knowledge won't always translate into immediate implementation. So I have three suggestions as you read this book:

1. **Use a journal as you read**. This book was not written for entertainment, although you might chuckle at my dry sense of humor as you read along. I really want you to find yourself in this book and use steps that will work for you. As you read, if you happen to come across transformational

pointers, write them down and answer the questions that I ask! Also write down things that really resonate with you as you read. Write down your feelings and everything that surfaces. This is how you track your growth.

2. **Share the principles that you learn with your sisters.** There are so many people who need to BREATHE. With your help, I can reach them. I've started the fire, but you have to help me to spread it. We need to spread this movement of healing and create a culture of self-discovery in women. We are the backbones of our societies, so no woman is exempt. Tell your co-workers, friends, strangers, your book club, social clubs, and your haters about this book. Share and do not spare! Connect with me on my website www.angelpdevone.com and make sure you leave your information so that we can keep in touch. You don't want to miss anything. Go to your social media accounts, create posts as you read along, and hashtag #breatheagain so that I can find you.
3. **Read the first chapter today.** YEP! Today. Jump right in! This book is not long at all. At least, I don't think so. The first three chapters are extensive in their information about God's original intention for your creation. There, you will learn the true source of your existence, and you will come out knowing who God is and why you are as phenomenal as you are. You can win in this thing called life. I invite you to the great life that is awaiting you. Remember, there is a little girl out there somewhere who is waiting on you to take your position. Just turn the page.

CHAPTER 1

The Power of Your Breath

"Most of us take the act of breathing for granted. In fact, many of us are barely aware of this miraculous process that takes place 24 hours a day, when we are awake and asleep. Without breath there would be no life."~ Anders Olsson

Since I can remember, I have always been someone who loves to be physically fit. The gym helps me to achieve this. The gym is one of those places I can visit even when I don't feel like it. It helps me decompress from stressful situations. I love going to the gym. I love all of the moving parts, from the people to the machines and free weights. I also love the sound of the weights clinking together or dropping onto the floor. Nowadays, gyms always seem to be crowded. Apparently, health and fitness are the new "things". Gym memberships are at an all-time high.

One day, I was in the gym working out, after all, I am on a mission to live my "best life" in real life. All the same, I am tired of using this phrase superficially in conversations or to make social media posts. I really want it to be my lifestyle, as it is becoming for many people. For me, what constitutes living the best life is actually going to the gym and working out, not pretending. I enjoy the pleasant feeling after a workout and the challenge that pushes me through the workout. Of course, my favorite benefits are the physical results that come with regular exercise; this include strength, muscular definition and increased energy. So, by no means am I going to let anyone or any circumstance come between my relationship with the gym. Maybe in the past, I would have, but at this point in my life, being physically fit is not an option. If I am being honest, I got tired of my New Year's resolution being "get fit". That resolution was on repeat every year. The average American makes the same New Year's resolution to start back working out or to work out consistently. NO MORE. My quality time with the gym is written with a pen into my weekly schedule.

Not only do I like to go to the gym, but I decided that I wanted a trainer as well. We all know the importance of exercising, but learning technique takes working out to a new level. This is where a trainer comes in. Their assignment is to create and demonstrate routines, assist clients in reaching fitness goals and keep people alive … literally. If you think about it, they always make sure you are aware of your breath. During workouts, they say things like, "Make sure you don't forget to breathe. Inhale through your nose; exhale through your mouth." It's like, they know when you are not doing it.

It was leg day at the gym when I told my trainer that I was ready to take my workout up a notch. I wanted to go hard. To this day, I don't know what I was thinking. If your trainer is anything like my trainer, you know that going hard is his motto. He is a maniac in the gym; it's almost as if he isn't human. He makes up insanity workouts in his sleep. He eats, sleeps and breathes health and fitness. So, by the time I realized what I'd said, it was too late to retract my words. So, I went with it. We hardly made it through the warm-up before I began panting. By the time we started our first round of leg exercises, I knew that my legs would feel like noodles in a matter of minutes. I was working extremely hard and I did not want to stop my workout, so I continued to push myself to the limit. All I could think about were the results. I should have been thinking about my breath. I was squatting with extremely heavy weights, and like clockwork, He would say in his insistent but sultry voice, "BREATHE." Every time he reminded me to breathe during the workout, I realized that I was not breathing. "How is this happening? I thought breathing could happen on its own. Breathing is involuntary. And how did he know that I was not breathing? Am I not privy to a gym secret, I thought?"

I guess the full importance and intentionality behind mindful breathing just never clicked with me. Since it's such a natural reflex, I never put any thought into it unless I was trying to overcome a panic attack, meditating or just deciding to take a few deep cleansing breaths to reset. We were born doing it. We can breathe without thinking about it. In my ignorance, I was amazed that such a thing as forgetting to breathe was possible. At that point, I was so enthralled with what was going on that I could do nothing for the rest of the workout but think about why my breathing kept stopping. I went home and conducted a Google search asking, "Why do I stop breathing while working out?" Apparently many other people had the same question, as it was a top search. I found out that, while it's natural to breathe, it's also natural to stop breathing when the body is exerting force, under pressure or when it is in deep concentration. This is especially true if no training on mindful breathing has ever been done. Most people do not know they are not breathing until the trainer says it or they pass out.

There had to be a reason beyond the physical that God was exposing this phenomenon to me. I've been involved with fitness for most of my life and such occurrence had never been so pronounced. This is what He revealed...my physical experience with breathlessness under pressure was a mirror of the world's psychological experience of breathlessness. As a generation, we are failing to do the very things that should be as normal as breathing. Under pressure, we settle, lose hope, show no resilience after a failure, become blind to our greatness, play small and leave our hearts open for ruin. Pressure has caused the world's mental and emotional pipes to burst. However, I took this revelation as a personal challenge to learn how to breathe physically, emotionally, spiritually and mentally so that I could use the pressure to create my best life.

After this day, I thought about breath a little differently. All of this time, I thought that it was okay just to let my breathing happen without thought, but what I learned is that to breathe without mindfulness is to live by chance. When breathing is threatened, every part of our being is threatened. Unfortunately, we are not always aware of our breath until it is indeed threatened. Breathing impacts every system, hence the reason it's so imperative to our overall health. Anders Olsson reports the following: "Inhaling is an active process in which our respiratory muscles are actively working to expand our chest so that air can enter. When we inhale, our heart beats faster (the pulse is raised) and the sympathetic part of the autonomic nervous system is activated. Exhalation is usually passive and does not require as much work. The diaphragm returns to its original position, and our thorax and lungs sink down without any muscle effort." (The Power of Your Breath, Olsson)

Whether focus is placed on proper breathing or not is the difference between just living and living the best life. Optimal breathing comes from mindful and controlled breathing. So, the implication is that in order for us to improve our breathing, which improves our lives, conscious attention and effort must be placed on proper breathing habits. And you are responsible for the quality of your life, therefore, you are responsible for how you breathe. At anytime, you are welcome to guide your breath.

You may ask, "Why do we take breathing for granted?" I think it's for the same reason we take other things for granted. We live under the influence of ignorance. All of these years, we have not been taught that there is a wrong and a right way to breathe, or that we even can control and improve our health with mindful breathing. The opportunity to live optimally is forfeited when ignorance is present. The power of your breathing is not connected to what you do automatically, but rather its conscious and controlled functionality. The same phenomenon is true for thinking. Thinking can be controlled just as breathing can be controlled. Unfortunately, we have not been aggressively seeking the strategies to improve either. For most of my life, I didn't spend any time monitoring my thoughts. Whenever a thought entered into my mind, I went with it. The external results manifested as poor decisions and poor behavior. My life was being controlled by my lack of control over my thoughts. During those years, I developed a lousy mindset and my mind was weak. Things that should have been natural for me to do based on my creation were hard. I gave away my power. I squandered opportunities. I did not have the heart to fight through certain challenges. All of my decisions were based on free-range thinking. I had no control over my thought-life, so I lacked consistency in my life. I didn't even know that I had the power to control my thoughts. This was a setup for passive living because thoughts will eventually become actions, words, moods, attitudes and objects. So, spending intentional time surveying and upgrading my mental real estate needed to become a practice. And the best way to practice this is to implement breathing exercises into your daily schedule. Ultimately, healthy breathing habits will increase happiness.

The discovery of identity is equivalent to understanding the power of your breath. You can "get your life" LITERALLY. This commands us to be present, engaged, aware and alive. But, in this superficial society in which we live, all deference has moved away from gaining deeper understanding and awareness of self to focusing on comparative living. Simply put, our modern culture does not cater to the proper way of living.

Your breath is full of sustenance and healing, as it is one of the body's most vital functions. Breath is the essence of life. Breathing can help you locate some of your problems so you can be on your way to a speedy recovery simply by changing your focus. Proper breathing is inhalation through the nose because the air is filtered and is said to help protect the body from viruses and other sickness. Breathing becomes difficult during extreme activity, like lifting weights. During inhalation, muscles are intensely engaged. This explains the breathlessness that I experienced while working out. Exhaling is the easy part breathing because it's expelling the air that came in through inhalation. Exhalation is the outward breath.

Everyday life has its ups and downs. Whether life seems to be up or down at any given time, I like to stay positive. In the midst of a crisis, we have learned a very common technique, one that now serves as a universal way of coping with strenuous situations. We simply tell the person who's under stress to take a deep breath. This simple but powerful instruction can save a life. This has become my ritual for getting through tough days. Conscious breathing altogether has greater benefits, but just being able to take a deep breath throughout the day has benefits of its own as well, and they are:

1. Attention- I've learned that taking a deep breath helps me to better manage my thoughts and prioritize the information entering my brain. When I take a deep breath in the midst of thoughts fighting for my attention, I am able to choose which piece of information to entertain.
2. Calmness - Taking a deep breath while experiencing an anxiety attack was very helpful and powerful. It's impossible to be calm and anxious at the same time. Breathing promotes calmness. My students benefit from taking deep breaths during emotional episodes.
3. Spiritual alignment - Breath carries God's Spirit, which holds His power. We all want and need power in our lives. Being empowered will always draw so many other things into our lives. And the Spirit within us enables us to do whatever God has made us to accomplish. The will of God is carried out by His Spirit.

There are a myriad of other benefits that come with taking deep breaths. A couple of those benefits include pain relief and blood pressure regulation.

Every task in life requires breath. If you are not breathing, you clearly are not doing anything. But in order to execute certain tasks properly, breathing must be emphasized. Therefore, breath awareness is vital. Day-to-day tasks do not necessarily require a focus on breath, but to sing, eat, deliver a baby, concentrate, or swim, breathing is always emphasized. I was even taking shooting classes with a navy seal, and part of our training included breathing techniques for better aim, timing and precision. While you may not concentrate too much on breathing on most days, practicing for giving is a must. I don't have children yet, but I've heard about the pain and discomfort involved. Breathing techniques are said to better manage labor pain over drugs. Relaxation is the best medicine for a complication-free delivery, but this is only achieved by using specific breathing techniques. Mothers will not be able to stay relaxed if their breathing is not controlled. "Breathing is the path through the contraction." ~Nicole Caccovo.

For a singer, correct breathing elongates the note. A masterful singer balances every note on the strength of the breath. They are great singers partly because of their mastery of proper breathing techniques.

Breathing is the secret to well-being—literally. Babies are the best at it. They take big deep breaths that fill their little stomachs, causing it to expand and flatten as they inhale and exhale. They don't have any external or internal stressors to prohibit them from breathing optimally. For this reason, they are masters of breathing. Growing and taking on responsibilities over time has the tendency to change our breathing patterns. I didn't know that it was so important to be so intentional about something that should seemingly come naturally, something that we have all been given. Having something and being aware of it are two completely different things.

Your physical breathing reveals what's going on internally. In other words, it's hinged upon your psychological well-being. Racing thoughts caused by anxiety might cause labored breathing and hinder your diaphragm function. While the body's breath is a mirror of its inner activity, practicing proper breathing techniques can soothe almost anything, including frustration and rage, thus creating a cycle of congruence. For this reason, health is so much more than just being physically fit.

A breath finalized our creation. The best part of God was transferred into you when He breathed His breath into Adam's nostrils. His breath accomplished some very important things that we've read about. The most obvious benefit is it provided life to Adam's spirit and soul. The breath of God parted the Red Sea and it put men back together again. The secret is out. Breath gives life, sustains life and resurrects life. That one workout made me realize that I needed better breathing habits spiritually, emotionally and naturally.

When I was researching for this book, I watched YouTube clips, read many articles, and attended workshops, but the most important information about natural breathing came from a book called, The Power of Your Breath by Anders Olsson. Mr. Olsson brilliantly confirmed everything that I'd spent years reading in all of the articles and other books I'd read. I also started to pay attention to my breath and make connections between my health and my breathing. After conducting polls and observing people from various demographics, and through research, my findings prove that very few people are living life at their best. We are unaware of our responsibilities and, for this reason, we are not taking advantage of our ability to improve our own lives. This level of living implies that those who are intentional, taking classes and investing in their lives have a better quality of life than others. Proper breathing of the soul is hinged on clarity. If you want your life to be stoic and mediocre, don't take any thought about your breathing habits, but if you want the power of your breath to be unlocked, let's breathe.

CHAPTER 2

Dare to be Different

I didn't have everything I wanted when I was growing up. My mother and my grandparents were all about providing my needs. I got some of the things that I wanted, but mostly on special occasions. What I did have was the most loving family and friends that anyone could wish for. I was blessed to be a healthy child. I had a place to lay my head every night after eating a hot dinner with my family, even though we did not eat all together the traditional way. The house was small enough that, even if we were not in the same room, we were close. I was also able to get an education. I was fortunate. Would I have enjoyed a few more toys? Yes! Would I have liked visiting more places, experiencing more outings? Yes! Would I have loved to have better clothes and shoes? Absolutely! But, I survived without it. After all, I believe children need to experience a different type of wealth that can't be given to them. It must be put inside of them. What I did not have in material wealth, my mom made sure I had in spiritual wealth. Rather than the most delicate of fabrics, I was given the lifelong belief that all of my needs would be divinely supplied. I didn't always have the latest pair of shoes, but God orchestrated my steps. It was because of the early exposure to spiritual identity that I came to believe that my life was in God's hands. That's real wealth. Wealth is not exclusively defined as having a big bank account and investments. Another form of wealth is having a stable family and having optimal health. So yes, I did have a silver spoon in my mouth. No, I wasn't birthed into any of the Hilton, Kardashian or Rockefeller familiesy, but depending on how you look at it, I was privileged to experience the upbringing that I did. A traditional silver spoon does not equate to having stability, love and support of a family. I would not trade my upbringing for any amount of money.

Family was and still is a major part of my life. My family is a very tightly-knit family and I like to think of us as a fun family. I joke about how news in my family spreads like wildfires. I'm not sure if that's a good or bad thing, but if you want something to be a secret in my family, it's better if you just keep it to yourself. My family has always been extremely supportive of my endeavors. There is no greater support system. They keep me grounded, and if I ever forget where I've come from, they will always remind me. This is especially true for my mom and my aunt. We need that from time to time.

"Remember who you are," Mom says. "You are a child of God. You can't do what everybody else does, and as long as you live in my house, you will not do what everybody else does." She often reminded me and my oldest brother that we live in the world, but we are not a part of the world's system. When I was a child, such statements sounded silly. I didn't understand them until I became an adult and finally began to think expansively about the concept of identity. This has nothing to do with anything that I can get from the world, but rather what I can offer to the world based on being a part of God's Kingdom.

"Dare to be different," was another one of my mom's mottoes. She used it frequently too, although back then, I didn't understand the point of being so "different". I just wanted to be as human as humanly possible. I was a kid; I wanted to do what other kids did and that's it, but sometimes, that was hard. I was just as different as my mom wanted me to be. I was concerned about things that most kids my age were not thinking about. I had insight into the things that were to come and I was sensitive to people's needs; I understood what people did not say. This made me weird and corny, and my peers were sure to express this. They literally told me, "You are weird." In high school, I was affectionately known as Grandma. At first, I thought it was an insult, but later realized it was a compliment. I could answer complex questions that adults asked, even at my young age, not all academic questions, just everyday life questions. I also loved to give advice, mediate hostile situations and empower people who seemed to have lost the awareness of their competence. This wasn't the main reason I was called Grandma. It was more so because I often told my friends what they should and should not do. When I think about it now, I grimace. We call that judging. No one wants to be judged. Hence, we have coined the phrase, "Don't judge me". I'd like to say that I did have an old soul. My old soul could be attributed to growing up in the house with my grandparents.

Although I was someone who did not fit in with groups or cliques, I certainly tried to fit in. I tried to fit in with the athletes. I tried to fit in with seniors when I was a freshman. I was all over the place. Later, I would discover that God made everyone different and He designed me and you to operate in the light of this uniqueness. We were never created to fit in. My mom apparently had a partnership with God as she did not allow us to think about comparing ourselves to others. She wanted to teach us to look at our own strengths. She wanted to teach us that our value is not based on the strengths or weaknesses of another person.

Royal Distinction

My mom did not hide her hatred of the world's system. As born again children of the Kingdom of Heaven, she wanted to make sure that we knew which one we belonged to. These are two completely different systems and ways of life. Let's be clear. She never wanted us to be snooty or think of ourselves as better than our peers; she simply wanted us to become okay with not accepting the world's standard. The honest truth is that none of us deserve citizenship in the Kingdom of God, so be aware of those who act as if they deserve everything that God gives them. Everything that we have has been provided to us based on an act of grace from our Creator. Such gift is not exclusive to me and my family alone. Anyone can gain access to the same Kingdom living. When Jesus became the highest ransom known to humanity, the framework was established for all people. All access is granted upon confession of sins and belief in Jesus as your personal Savior. This is all about relationship. The destination has never been religion, contrary to what we thought growing up. Once Jesus is given permission to shape the lives of those who believe, He supplies a fresh breath of air that invigorates the soul that was once lost. Have you ever come in contact with someone and that person's presence brought a breath of fresh air? Jesus has the same effect, but with a greater magnitude. Life begins, and after this, you have been adopted into royalty. You are no longer subjected to the world's paradigm.

I want you to know, similar to how my mom wanted us to know, you live in the world, but you don't have to accept what the world offers. You can operate in a fundamentally different manner. In the world's kingdom, the aim is to control your behavior. In God's Kingdom, the aim is to mold you into the image of God inside and outside. In the world, the focus is on religion, background, and worldly ideologies, but in God's Kingdom, the aim is to replicate God's love. You get the point. Another way to look at it is royal kings and queens learn at an early age that they are different and must not partake in the same practices or have the same mindset as the world at large. The same is true for the kings and queens of God's Kingdom. There are two systems that are distinct in that they function uniquely and are shown in the structure of our lifestyles. Look at it like this. When Kate married Prince William, she became Princess Kate; her name changed (quite naturally) and so did her citizenship. She is now a member of the Royal family. In a sense, a certain aspect of her identity changed. One definition of identity is simply "the name of a person." Princess Kate gave up her normal life to embrace a life of servitude. That's what happens once we accept Jesus into our lives. Our names change, we gain citizenship into the Kingdom of Heaven and we give up what would have been a normal life in exchange for a life of servitude. We respond to evil with good, and we pray for our enemies. We don't heap up goods and materials for ourselves; we give and we share.

In her new lifestyle, everything Princess Kate says, eats, drinks and wears and does cannot mirror the speech or behavior she was accustomed to before she became a royal. This means something significant. In the same manner that Princess Kate received a name change and her life was upgraded, our names are changed and our lives are upgraded when we receive Christ. Certainly, she counted the cost of what she had to give up before the decision was made. Ultimately, Kate gained so much more than she gave up.

My childhood friends remind me to this day that my mom was not playing games. Ironically enough, when I tried to act up at school, only remembering my mom's mottoes about identity helped me to better manage my behavior. It helped me to identify who I was as a child of the King and as a child of Angela Lockwood. If I am being honest, it stopped me in my tracks because I did not want my mom to show up at school. As an adult, I still pull on those mottoes that I now call confessions of my identity. They help me to make it through certain situations that test my confidence, self-esteem, resilience, and my strength. There is no way to guarantee that childhood influences success as an adult. But, I embrace the high and low points of my upbringing as I can point to several factors that have helped me to get through rough times. I reach back into my childhood often to find courage and strength for my adult challenges.

The dictionary defines identity in several different ways. The first definition is "the fact of being who or what a person or thing is" (Oxford Dictionary). I love this definition and you will come to understand why later in this chapter as I reveal how my name helped me in my identity discovery process. The second definition of identity, which comes from the Cambridge Dictionary, is "the qualities of a person that make them unique and different from others." Although not as succinct in its length, I love the latter definition. To sum it all up in my own words, identity is a positive awareness of self, whether it's created or discovered. When I first read this definition, it pointed me back to what my mom told me as a child to shape my behavior. "Know who YOU are" and "Dare to be different." In my opinion, it just amplifies over the first definition. Additionally, it suggests that even beyond having a distinct and unique name, everyone is able to do something special. It also suggests that every single person has a set of qualities that makes that person different from ANY other person that has or will ever exist. With almost eight billion people on the planet, we know that there are people who share our same skills and talents. However, no one has what you have the way you have it. No combination or implementation is the same. Each of us can do something that no one else can do. God put His brilliance on display during your creation. Exclusivity still exists, even in similarities. You are wholly unique.

The great thing about definition two is that it gives clarity to the unique combination of strengths, skills and experiences that will enable every individual to recognize their value, as well as to create value. When identity is realized, there is a greater recognition and appreciation of our differences, strengths, abilities, and frailties. Even though there are some things that you can't do, there are several other things that you can do that no one else can imitate.

The authenticity of identity is declining in a world that has become a melting pot of unhealthy competition, comparison and facades. A weakened identity is the root cause of most personal struggles that people face. It can either help us move forward or hold us back. This is why we all must commit to self-discovery before our time here on Earth expires. We must aggressively pursue such achievement together. Even those on a mission to change the world, the rich and the famous, must not lose sight of the man staring back in the mirror. That person has to be developed also because changing the world starts from within. In many cases, ordinary people idolize celebrities as if the obligation of self-discovery is beyond them. The problem is that talent, gifts and achievements can sometimes be mistaken as self-discovery, especially when people can professionally hide bad character behind gifts. Understanding gifting is only one aspect of self-discovery. While many entertainers have certainly found their gift, self-discovery is the ability to manage life's experiences more effectively. This includes having the courage to be honest about your emotional status and accepting moments when challenges exceed your natural ability to cope. Some of the most successful people I know are honest with themselves about what they need.

Let's Go Back

We can take a walk down memory lane and see that this world has been blessed to experience the gifts of some very extraordinary entertainers. Obviously, inherent ability is not relegated to just entertainers. You may have seen within your family, circle or industry that people are extremely talented. However, some are simply without hope. People have silent contemplations that lead to the unfortunate act of suicide. Not only that, some self-medicate to cope with the anxieties of success. It has been so clearly pronounced that success does not always come wrapped in a pretty package. As a result, people like Michael Jackson, one of my favorite actors, Robin Williams, and fashion icon, Kate Spade, all experienced tragic endings because of their inability to manage success or see their full greatness.

Once realized and activated, the discovery of identity has the power to be the greatest asset known to humanity, because of its intense capability to impact every segment of our lives. With identity-discovery or self-discovery (the two words can be used interchangeably), uniqueness is fair game. You can be confident without being insensitive, become a millionaire and help others do that same. You can take responsibility for what transpires in your life without blaming others, and you can eliminate fear and misery in your life. Identity-discovery is the beginning of all success.

People are living in paralyzing fear, searching for happiness outside of themselves in material possessions, power, jobs, accomplishments, wealth and relationships, among many other things—things and realities that can change in the blink of an eye and are not a reflection of authentic identity. Positions and titles given by people can be taken, bank accounts decrease and material things can fade and depreciate in value. While some define themselves by things that can be taken in the blink of an eye, the essence of who you have the ability to become is forever before you. You were uniquely designed, and this does not change. The time has come for you to unleash that uniqueness. If you guessed that the process starts with self-discovery, you are right. Knowing or not knowing who you are will become evident in your life's choices. Research shows that your thinking influences your expression of who you are, such as your conversations, your responses to various life circumstances and your personality. Basically, your belief about who you are will play a role in your behavior.

Every teenage girl will find herself spinning in the hallway, trying to find her way. “Which group of girls should I sit with? If I wear this, will they like me? What If I don’t really want to go to the mall with them after school? What if they find out that I love God and I go to church every Sunday? What if they find out that I am a “straight A” student who loves to read books?” This line of questioning is normal. We all seek acceptance, but later in life, we find that the acceptance we are looking for is really self-acceptance. Furthermore, self-discovery is all about completely eliminating external influences and getting in touch with our own personal greatness.

Whether you are a teenager in high school battling the pull of pop culture and peer pressure, a middle aged woman fighting the sting of rejection after a recent divorce, a woman trying to push past failure, or a person who wants to embrace your inherent abilities, self-discovery is the foundation of peace. Your awareness of who you are will help you make even more discoveries about yourself in every segment of your life and will help you pull through the toughest of times in life. Sometimes, you may need a counselor, coach, a mentor or even an accountability partner, but all of these tools are available to you. Sometimes you might just need to remember a prior victory for encouragement. What I know for sure is that you have what you need inside of you. It is waiting to be unearthed and utilized. Your real strengths come into play when your instincts come rushing in to save your life. You have been given struggles that are customized to reveal your strengths. Experts are experts because they've all failed at some point. John Maxwell said it this way, "The more you do, the more you fail. The more you fail, the more you learn. The more you learn, the better you get." You have been given strengths that are customized to the struggles that you face. That's why each of our lives are so unique and necessary. None of us experience life the same way growing up. That's with intention. It's almost like we are living in different worlds, but we have traits and experiences uniquely crafted for our own personal cxperiences.

While there is a difference between our natural and the spiritual identities, the two are connected by one element: breath. Your natural existence is your soul, and your soul consists of your mind, will, and emotions. Your spiritual being is the part of you that connects with God. Your physical breath is how your body remains alive. All were activated by God's breath. The identity of your soul is as vital as the breath in your body. Controversially, it is the single most essential element of successful navigation through the life-experience. If we took a pole and asked, "What is the one element you can't live without?" the responses would vary, but breath should be the number one answer. After all, it's mostly related to both forms of existence. Some will say food, water, success, love, expression, sex and so on, but if we talk through the answers, we can eliminate several responses by deducing the most accurate. Love is powerful, but it cannot be used to resuscitate a dying person. Doctors are unable to feed a person their favorite food to make them live again. The kitchen does not contain anything that will sustain life; the same is true for water. I can bring the ocean to your front door, but if you are not breathing to consume the water, you will not and cannot drink it. For this reason, breath is the most essential element of life. Essentially, our souls are who we are at our core. It's what we would do or think before we ask, "What would Jesus do?"

I have heard people say that success is an inside job. Indeed it is, but the inside job is discovering your inner wiring—this is is the wiring that will aid in your success. Without it, no one will understand or have his or her own definition of success, thus making it impossible to achieve anything on a consistent basis. Consequently, we will look to others to define what success looks like. Some will depend on others to set the standard for them, others will not value their own gifts and skills enough to pursue their passions. Neither you nor I were made to achieve success based on an external meaning of what success should look like. True success can only be achieved by the one who knows the reason they were created and put on Earth. That individual will love himself or herself enough to work towards the completion of that purpose because he or she will understand what makes him or her necessary. Purpose can only be unveiled by taking the steps to dissect everything about self and learn the many different layers to self. Similarly, the most important person who we should desire to meet is ourselves. Once we get to know ourselves, we can throw away the need to live according to the pictures that people have painted for us and the expectations that they have of us.

Features of Natural Identity

Genealogy is a description of what traits we have inherited from our parents and even our great-grandparents. Have you ever heard an older person in your family say something like, "You look just like your grandmother?" They are simply recalling your genetic makeup. Interestingly enough, we don't just get our physical traits from our mothers and fathers, but we sometimes get our personality traits from them as well.

An interesting element of identity is *chronology*. I am the second-born child of my parents. Needless to say that I have defied that odd. Although, I have had hardships like everyone else, I am not doomed to a life of trouble. I was the baby for almost twelve years before my reign came tumbling down after the birth of my baby brother, Emmanuel, followed by the birth of my sister, Denisha. The attention almost always transfers to the youngest and rightfully so, after all, they need the most attention … in a sense. My mom never stopped being an exceptional mother. She loved us all the same, but I think most children naturally feel the shift that takes place when a new sibling enters the scene.

Geography is all about where a person lives during their childhood experience. Believe it or not, the environment where you were raised has the ability to influence your behavior and your beliefs. Childhood environmental conditions whether ideal or not, can reflect in your personality. When food, water and clothing are scarce, people learn to be grateful for everything. Consequently, they can become more prone to a scarcity mindset. In developed countries like the USA, we are wasteful, and as a result, we are ungrateful because we believe we'll always have everything we'll need to get by. The environment can take part of the blame.

Does any of this play a part in your life's development or define your destiny? Yes, but not entirely! They just provide enough information to sustain us until we learn more of the truth. For years, people thought that their genes or the environment in which they were raised determined their capabilities. Of course, we bought into this idea because we tend to depend on the highest level of information we are exposed to. We are no wiser than what we have been programmed to believe by our teachers, spiritual leaders and the world's leaders. If we don't become curious enough to study beyond a lecture, we will die without the opportunity to explore what we could become. Many of our ancestors had to overcome substantial hardships throughout their lifetimes. Just knowing that they had great inner strength to endure can be a powerful motivator for those of us trying to understand our places in the world. I often reflect on the inherent strength that my grandparents describe when I talk to them. One of my deepest desires is to have the strength and the courage of that generation.

Genes, contrary to what some doctors say, do not predict limitations or determine success. Sometimes, our inability to achieve a good outcome is based on limited knowledge. While all of the above factors may contribute to the formation of personality, no factor determines your success or health. Although our genetic makeup accounts for some personality traits, our genes, geography or chronology alone do NOT determine how our lives will play out. Your ability to make decisions is transformative in itself.

How do we determine that the success or failure was the result of chronology or genealogy? I believe that we can align our decisions with the desired results. So, you are not a victim of either factor, because your success is inextricably linked to your decisions. The potential for your life to take the form of the environments, genes, and chronology is only the result of lack of exposure to a higher level of truth. For example, we all believed the fundamental law of gravity until the law or aerodynamics came about explaining to us how airplanes stay suspended in the air. New levels of exposure increase our capability. Whether potential is negative or positive, it's not guaranteed. We all have the potential to succeed, but does this mean that we will? NO! When we learn that potential is not a guarantee, we are exposed to a greater level of wisdom, and this shifts our perspective. We also have God who provides the best definition about our make-up and outcome.

The Importance of Clarity

The journey through the stages of life lead to some very difficult circumstances. I have come to learn that it's just a part of living. Likewise, knowing what makes you unique helps your brain create answers that will guide you through the circumstances. The journey to self-discovery starts with clarity. As you hone in and gain clarity on who you are, you will simultaneously develop the courage to remove anything hat does not align with who you are. It also helps you to accept who you are not.

The process will not yield perfect results. For all of us, we sometimes find dichotomy between who we are versus our behavior. Your responsibility is to choose to allow who you are to lead. Only then will you be able to change your behavior. If you don't think you can do this, deeper exploration of subconscious activity is needed. We will need to change the fixed mindset you have about yourself. Your view has to be expanded through exploration of the truth. I recommend the Bible to supplement the process. With the Bible as my roadmap, I know that the path that I have chosen is well lit and holds proven transformation. I've been able to understand what God accomplished through the transference of His breath into Adam. Adam is a representation of all of us. This spiritual transference provided us with our identities. I can't determine your reality, so even if you don't believe in God or Jesus, the Bible has several principles that can be extracted and applied to the journey. You will learn them as the book progresses. Once you have identified and committed to developing the qualities and attributes that make up the elements of your identity, the possibility for you to live the best and most dominating life will be boundless.

Would you like to create a fulfilled life, which warrants mental clarity to communicate a message to yourself and others that you are serious about something? Quite frankly, you need this type of influence. In life, people don't buy what you sell them or what you tell them, they buy who you are. So, it goes without saying that if you don't know who you are, no one else will. "Perhaps people may be confused about who you are because you are." ~Dr. Cindy Trimm.

Business and Identity

If Steve Jobs, as the leader of one of the greatest organizations in history, could not clearly articulate the identity of his company and why it exists beyond its products and services, how could he expect to gain a customer base, attract employees, or even grow in capability? I would ask a similar question to politicians. While racing to hold an office they exchange derisive opinions, slander, and ridicule. Sadly, some use manipulation to gain a political following. This seems absurd to most because of the ignorance of any political issues, not to mention the lack of decorum to lead properly. Without going on a political rant from my political perspective, often candidates have been unsuccessful at clearly articulating who they are outside of being wealthy. I am convinced that there is a disparity in self-knowledge and their personal reason for pursuing a political office is unknown. Consequently, constituents are left to guess and assume that the candidates are capable of performing the job at hand. Leading in this magnitude first requires self-discipline. So, if a politician is unable to articulate the reason for seeking office outside of the obvious "to serve the public", how will voters know who to follow?

We live in the age of "FOLLOW ME." Many want to be followed for one reason or another, but few have the ability to lead properly. Manipulation has now become the catalyst and the standard for developing a following in many sectors, such as relationships, politics, religion and media..., among several other factors. Nevertheless, one thing that I have found is that manipulative people are unable to persuade those who know them and are settled in the truth. True influence is gained by an individual's willingness to follow the leader, not through bribery. It requires those who are leading to be clear about their identity without being manipulative, and those who are following to believe and agree with whomever it is that they are following. Even in a disagreement, the art of respect is not lost and manipulation is not used because, "disagreement does not mean disloyalty." ~Apostle Bryan Meadows. It is impossible to support an individual without disagreeing with some of their concepts, perspectives and theories. Everyone is entitled to have and voice his or her own opinion. Only those who thrive on control want everyone to agree with everything they do and say. This individual is relegated to frailties and will never grow outside of his or her own personal limitations.

Your Name Might Be Linked To Your Assignment

My name, Angel, is not a very common name. However, it holds a very strong universal meaning. Even without believing in God or Heaven, most people have heard of angels. Angels are usually known as messengers and guards, but they are not limited to those two assignments. Angels are divinely assigned by God to do things that people can't do for themselves. They even protect people from unseen danger. In the Bible, some are guardians, some provide supernatural insight and understanding, while others fight and are constantly looking to help us in any way possible. Just because my name is Angel does not automatically mean that I take on the nature of a divine angel. However, I believe that my name being Angel prophetically links me to my purpose. I am honored to know that my life as God's servant is in keeping with the assignment of His heavenly beings. When it comes to my name, I am responsible for the image that people perceive. My goal is to live up to my name and I take it very seriously.

"Your brand is your name, basically. A lot of people don't know that they need to build their brand; your brand is what keeps you moving"-Meek Mill

When we start to look at identity, we can refer to names, in some cases. In the next chapter, we will discuss the names of God. Remember, one of the definitions of identity is the name of a person. Perhaps, there is no universal meaning for your name, and that's okay. Now, your job is to make a name for yourself in such a way that people will associate your name with something great. In business, it's called personal branding. Even people who don't use Apple products have something good to say when the brand is the topic of discussion. Maybe this is just my biased opinion. When people call your name, what kind of connections are they making? What feelings and memories populate their mind? Think about some of our world leaders or just some influential person you have a personal connection with. When you hear that person's name, what associations can be made? When you hear names such as Martin Luther King, Bill Gates, Miley Cyrus, Oprah Winfrey,

Nelson Mandela, Jesus Christ, Beyonce, Michelle Obama, Adolf Hitler or Donald Trump, what do you immediately think? I know this list just took your mind from one extreme to the next. More often than not, your identity is attached to your name, as the definition suggests. What do you want your name to be associated with?

"A good name is rather to be chosen than great riches and loving favor rather than silver and gold." Proverbs 22:1

God created you to have a unique power, characteristics and purpose. However, He designed us to also have small levels commonality with our lives through His will. When we discover our true spiritual identity, we all draw closer to Him. As believers, we get to use the Bible as a manual to understand more about our identities in Christ and how not to lose sight of who we are created to be. I believe you have good traits that you can extract from your heritage that inform the good qualities you see in yourself today. My grandmother died in 2016, and at her funeral, I learned so much about her. These discoveries helped me to better understand the strengths that I can access. Natural heritage has its advantages. Sitting at the service provoked me to draw strength from my lineage and my natural identity and orient myself as a relatable human being. I learned to take pride in my heritage as a Black woman with no shame. And I actually felt a push to take my place in the world. My grandmother created opportunities for herself as a southern citizen. She worked for everything that she had. No handouts were available to her. Not too far removed from growing up in the Depression, every nickel she earned was precious. She always had a money saving tip, and she did pretty well for herself. She was strong, witty and feisty, even in her last days. Five things that I learned from my grandmother (Lucy P. Murray) in particular are:

1. Pay your bills on time every month.
2. Invest in land.
3. Age does not hinder development.
4. Appreciate your health and be thankful

5. Cherish every minute that you have with family and friends.

As much as I learned from her while she lived, her strength is what I think about in times when I may feel defeated or inadequate. Remembering who you are daily will provide a sturdy foundation for responding to day-to-day obstacles because it speaks to how we do life, how we look at life and how we respond to what happens in life. But like everything, this is a process. The development of identity starts early and must be developed throughout every phase of life. A good life can become great with the discovery of who we are. Just that knowledge of spiritual and natural heritage from my mom's daily departure speeches helped to shape my behavior and caused me to be calculated in my thinking.

The key to navigating the journey of identity discovery is to identify personal characteristics, optimizing innate capabilities and building on them. Otherwise, like myself, you can be incapacitated by fear and stuck in the same repetitive thought patterns for over a decade, never learning to navigate the unknown. One of my favorite concepts of self-discovery is that it provides the permission to completely eliminate external influences from your decision-making process, thus, allowing you to be honest with yourself. Thankfully, there are ways to eliminate the feelings of comparison, jealousy and others from your life. It's from my own personal account of failures, more failures and finally a track of wins that I have created this list for making self-discovery a priority. Feel free to add your own reasons to this list. While not exhaustive, this list an excellent way to start and end effectively.

Here are 13 Reasons to Make Self Discovery a Priority:

1. Your spiritual and personal needs will be met. As one of the most vital parts of your being, your spirit needs significant amounts of care. Since you are responsible for your spirit, it becomes your job to assess your needs and place your attention there. Fulfilling your spiritual needs in turn strengthens your psychology and body.

It's not until you have taken care of your own needs that you can dedicate yourself to changing lives. If your needs are abandoned, you can risk losing everything over time.

2. You'll get to know one of the greatest people alive and that is YOU!! You are one of God's most amazing creations. You came into this world with a great level of wisdom and creativity. Your personal knowledge of this truth opens up a world of new possibilities for your life. When you focus on self-discovery, you might really start to love the person you are getting to know.
3. You can carry an authentic message. Authenticity allows you to tap into a flow of unexplained joy. There is something liberating about being able to live with no pressure to perform. This level of freedom came from taking the time to understand my wiring and not trying to live outside of that revelation.
4. You'll save money, effort and time. I wasted so much money going to college to pursue a bachelor's degree that I don't even use. To this day, I have never taken a class that helped me recover from a failure or become a better person. It's ironic that we choose majors and careers before we choose ourselves. In doing so, there is a tendency to lose connection with who we are. I would have been able to choose or even create work that was in alignment with who I am, had I known.
5. You will not allow comparison and jealousy to stifle your growth. Comparison is a slap in the face to God. It sends Him the message that He did not do well enough when He made you. Viewing yourself through the eyes of comparison will always cause you to feel dispensable and inferior. When you know who you are, you finally come to terms with your greatness. As a result, you create something commendable that both you and God can be proud of. There is no need to compare yourself to others who are doing great when you realize that greatness is a built into your life.

6. Your Emotional Quotient (EQ) will increase. This simply means that you can recognize your emotions within a situation. Rather than reacting, you can use the emotion as information, and then choose how you want to respond. Discovering that you have emotions and emotions don't have you will minimize emotional craziness. Fear will be a non-factor and you will make non-emotional decisions.
7. You won't settle for less. Being convinced of something makes it extremely difficult to be swayed another way. When you know who you are and what you want, you are too stubborn to take any less than what you desire. PERIOD!
8. You will gain clarity on who God is. Self-discovery can seem like God is being left out because of its emphasis on "I". But, it's not without the God-factor. The truth is that self-discovery requires God. Without discovering who God is, there is no self-discovery. Everything we are is based on who God is. We are created in His image. Therefore, every time we get a chance to say I, it should reflect who God says we are.
9. Decision-making is so much easier. Decisions are harder without wisdom, self-knowledge and vision. Knowing who you are means knowing what you want. With this knowledge, you will make decisions that are in alignment with your destiny.
10. Solutions are emphasized over problems. When I experienced adversity at a young age, I was blinded to my strengths and I lost the awareness of my charisma and my competencies. As a result, I made excuses for myself because of the problems that were created. Once I discovered the real me, a new world of resources and answers from within opened up to me.
11. You will revive your mental health and ultimately, your life. Before your life reaches a destination, your mind has to be the first to get there or else you will not go. Consequently, when life happens, your mental health

can take the hardest blow. It can cause self-esteem to plummet and distort your once positive view of yourself. As a result, you may live based on those conditions, rather than becoming who you are destined to be. With your mind, your life can be revived and put back onto its designed path.

12. When life gets tough, you will persevere and stay the course. We will all experience tough times in life. That's just the way it is. You are scheduled to go through difficulties. That's not to say that success is impossible or that you will be a product of the difficult experiences. In fact, every difficult situation builds muscle to successfully face the next new challenge. So, rather than becoming the product of the difficult experiences, you become the product of the strength you gained, and from there, you can bombard your way through.
13. You are able to create a more powerful and attractive version of yourself. When I decided to be vulnerable and tell my story of shame, a miracle happened. That is, I stopped defining myself based on misconceptions that I drew from past experiences. I was able to create my identity from a clearer and truer perspective.

The inheritance associated with identity discovery is LIFE. Your close attention to who you are and what you offer promotes the satisfaction of a job well done. You won't need to seek approval or compare yourself to others ever again. Part of the answer is recognizing your full ability and embracing all that comes with it. This was given to you. Your identity is your promise and your weapon. God knows who you are apart from any other. You have royal distinction, and this gives you access to all that you will ever need as you pursue purpose.

My hope is that you can find yourself somewhere between my struggles and my victories, apply what you find and get results.

I am committed to sharing my knowledge and living by my convictions to also share my failures.

CHAPTER 3

I Am

"You are who you are and what you are because of what has gone into your mind. You can change who you are and what you are by what goes into your mind." –Zig Ziglar

Self-discovery is an essential element of developing an intimate relationship with yourself. This book is about working with God to create that experience. Although scriptures will be mentioned throughout the book, my prayer is that you will be introduced to yourself and God all over again. I also pray that you have the courage to remove people from the process. The chosen scriptures are answers that God wants us to have from His heart. They are readily available. I was able to gather that if I knew how to accurately identify God for myself, my revelation of who He is would help me to answer the infamous question of "Who am I?" And it did. This has nothing to do with religion. So, let's park right here with this question, "Who is God?" Well, I don't think that I have the words to adequately describe God and His glory. Even with all of the cute words of praise, our limited knowledge still comes up short when trying to define someone so honorable.

God is multifaceted and there are many layers to His nature. His complexity requires that people conduct extensive research to understand fully. In Exodus 3:14, the first time that He gets the opportunity to introduce Himself, He wanted to make it simple for Moses, so He told him, "I AM THAT I AM, and I WILL BE WHAT I WILL BE." In other words, God was saying to Moses, I AM *everything* that you will need in order to accomplish the assignment that I have given you. I AM your strength and I AM your confidence to speak what I have commanded you to speak. I AM your protection against Pharaoh and I AM able to take care of any concerns you may have regarding setting the Israelites free.

God, in His brilliance, has many ways to help us understand who He is. In the various stories of the Bible, He finds ways to reveal His attributes by telling us specific truths about Himself. While the I AM is a name that God gave Himself, the Names of God were given by people in the Bible to commemorate a significant act that He performed on their behalf. The names serve the purpose of helping readers understand His power and learn how to expand that knowledge. Nothing creates a more intimate relationship than learning the intricacies of a person. As we were created to worship and bring glory to God, knowing His names help us know what He is like and provide insight as to how and why we worship Him.

The remainder of this chapter is a breakdown of 11 of the names of God. Let's put His names in perspective.

THE NAMES OF GOD

I don't claim to know Hebrew, other than the few words that I learned from having Jewish friends and my mom's godparents. They were Jewish as well. Other than that, I study the Hebrew meanings of words that I want to know the deeper meaning of. Hebrew is one of the original languages of the Bible; it was the language that God used to communicate. Sometimes, it can be restrictive when I really want to know what God said or who He is. So, I just search out the translation of the original language. With the words that I have studied, a whole new world has opened up for me. Hopefully, by the time you finish reading this chapter, you will have a similar experience. I still recommend deeper study of these words and any others in their original language as you may receive a different understanding.

The names of God are Hebrew names. You will find that Jehovah or El precede His names. It's a respect thing, similar to the way El precedes masculine words in Spanish. Used alone "El" means God, but when used in conjunction with other words, will take on a different meaning. This is similar to prefixes being added to a root word in English. The El or Jehovah prefixes create new meaning. Remember, we are talking about the same God, just learning His various powers. Each power is identified by a name that we call a "name of God". When Jehovah is used alone, it also means God. In the Bible days, it was illegal to use the name "God". From this law, we have coined the commandment, "Don't use the name of the Lord in vain." His name is holy, sacred and should only be used if it was needed. Using the name in a random conversation was considered a form of disrespect. The fear of God actually included not mentioning His name at all, outside of a prayer.

Some theologians have argued about the correct pronunciations of Hebrew names. My goal is not to continue or end the argument, but to simply explain my findings in an empowering way. More than pronunciation, we should know God through a relationship with Him. We will forfeit the opportunity to know God if we lessen our relationship with Him to the correct pronunciation of His Hebrew name. Plus, I don't think He will be mad or ignore us if we mispronounce one of His names. There are so many ways to spell each of them; you might see a spelling different from what you have seen. I chose the spellings that were the most common.

ELOHIM

When God steps onto the scene in Genesis, we are introduced as *ELOHIM.* "In the beginning, God (Elohim) created the heavens and the earth" (Genesis 1:1). This particular name introduces our God and our Father as a supernatural creative. During the next few chapters, God's highlight tape starts. He created everything. He created you and me, plants animals, stars, sun, Heaven, Earth and the moon. If you consider yourself a creative, this should light up your life and trigger you to tap into your creative nature. Your Father is a creative. His creative mind is intrinsic to this name. If you have ever wanted to know where you get your creative ability from, here it is. It came through your mom and/or your dad, but God is the original source.

JEHOVAH ROHI

Even if you have never stepped foot in a church, you might have heard someone say, “The Lord is my Shepherd.” This based on one of the most familiar names of God, Jehovah Rohi. “The original or Hebrew word for Shepherd is *ROHI”* (Ramsay, 2017). The 23rd book of Psalms put Jehovah Rohi on the map when David was describing his experience with God. God was showing David that he was similar to God. David was described as a man after God’s heart because they were so much alike. With respect to their functions, as David was to the sheep, God is to us. As God’s sheep, we learn to trust Him because He is so faithful to take care of our needs and keep us safe. In the same way, David met the needs of the sheep. I believe that David was called “the Shepherd Boy” because he was exemplifying the same strengths as “The Great Shepherd”. As long as the sheep had David, they had enough. God desires to be Jehovah Rohi to you. He wants to tend to you as David did the sheep. He desires a personal relationship with you, something that religion can’t provide.

Scripture references for Jehovah Rohi: Ezekiel 34:11-15, Genesis 48:15, Genesis 49:24, Psalm 80:1.

ADONAI

ADONAI. “This name of God means Lord” (Ramsay, 2017). It emphasizes God's Lordship. The best way to understand this name is to think about a landlord. He is the owner of property. Like a landlord owns property, God owns us. There is only one difference. That is, we never have to worry about our property value decreasing. Through His Lordship, He holds a preeminent place in our lives… first in order, first in rank and first in importance. However, He never forces His way into our lives. Only when given the opportunity, He rules our lives, orders our steps and we are open to His chastisement. Having the breath of

God stresses our calling to a relationship with God as our Owner and Provider. No other creation has His breath. Similarly, none of them have the connection that we have with Him.

Scriptures for reference: Exodus 34:23, Gen 15:2, Exodus 20:7.

EL ELYON

One of my favorite names for God is the name *EL ELYON*. It is taken from a root word that means "to go up". It's literal meaning is "Most High God" (Ramsay, 2017). As you know, God is in every place. When I was a little girl, we sang a song that says, "The Lord is high above the Heavens." So, that means if He lived somewhere traceable by GPS, it would be higher than anything we can see. Secondly, His name has more power than any other name that exists. This power expressly causes all of creation to recognize His high and majestic position. No other name can save, heal, cause the dead to live again, or cause enemies to be delivered into their hands.

Many gods exist on Earth, but all of them bow to the highest name, El Elyon. This is my favorite name for God because it comes from Psalm 91, my favorite chapter in the book of Psalms. It says, "He that dwells in the secret place of the Most High (El Elyon) will rest in the shadow of the All Mighty".

Scripture references: Genesis 14:18 Genesis 14:19, Genesis 14:20 Genesis 14:22, Psalm 57:2, Psalm 78:35.

EL SHADDAI

Men and women alike are made in the image of God. This name took on a whole new meaning when I realized that my inner working to rescue, counsel and nurture those around me was based on my spiritual makeup. God designed women with breasts so that we can fulfill the role of nourishing our children. This goes to show that God gave us all the tools to complete our assignments. In the same way that our physical breath parallels the breath of our soul, our physical design is the perfect parallel of our spiritual mandate. *EL SHADDAI* is the name of God that is reflective of His nature to supply, protect, nourish, satisfy, comfort and provide. El Shaddai is interpreted as "The All-Sufficient One" (Ramsay, 2017). I've also seen it interpreted as "God Almighty". El Shaddai is not only where the ability to complete your assignment comes from, but He is also where your blessings, nourishment and provision come from. You serve a nurturing God who will not allow your needs to go unmet.

Scripture references: Genesis 17:1, Genesis 28:3, Genesis 35:11, Genesis 43:14, Genesis 48:3

JEHOVAH M'KADDESH

We have an unrivaled God, Creator and Father who holds all power. With such a God on our side, we can't go wrong. Well, we can go wrong but He gives us the opportunity to make it right. He stands alone in His class to make us holy. He created you to share the same accolade. So, Jehovah *M'KADDESH* sanctifies you and makes you holy, as the definition "The Lord Who Sanctifies" suggests. I hope this news is as good to you as it was for me. I tried for years to do the job of Jehovah M'Kaddesh, but to no avail. It's like trying to save yourself. GIVE UP. You can't do it. God alone holds that power. Adhering to the law will not do it. The Word of God has made it clear that we will have shortcomings and will not always do everything right. We will sin. PERIOD! God does not like sin, but He loves the sinner, so He provides grace. This name of God is grace at its best. When you begin to see yourself as special as God sees you, you will accept His grace. By His grace, you are sanctified.

Scripture references: Exodus 31:13 Leviticus 20:8

EL ROI

The Bible has been my most reliable resource in regards to the transformation that my life has taken. If that is not enough to encourage you to read the Bible, here is a better one. The Bible is filled with epic stories with superheroes, poetry, parables, fights and drama. YES DRAMA! Reality television does not compare to the stories of the Bible. I mean this in the most reverential way. I love the Bible. You may find it hard to believe that this next story came from the Bible.

The name *EL ROI* is given to the Lord in Genesis 16:13 by a woman named Hagar. She gave this name to Him because He saw and heard her when she thought no one was there. For her, El ROI meant "God who sees".

"And she called the name of the Lord that spoke unto her, Thou God seest me: for she said, Have I also here looked after him that seeth me? (Genesis 16:13 KJV)

Prior to this verse, Hagar, whose name means, "one who seeks refuge", became pregnant by Abraham with the permission of his wife, Sarah. At the time, Hagar was working for them. Of course, they still wanted Hagar to work for them after conception. WAIT!! So, Hagar was pregnant by a woman's husband and after becoming pregnant, had to go submit under the wife's authority? The answer is YES. I know what you are thinking:

1. Is this REALLY in the Bible?
   AND
2. Did Hagar go back to Abraham and Sarah's house?

Yes, she did because she wanted to obey God. After Hagar became pregnant, Sarah became jealous of her and held Hagar in contempt for following the instructions that she had given her. Her attitude towards Hagar became resentful. Hagar could not bear the hate and did what most women would have done. She quit and left. Unfortunately, the only place she had to go was to the desert. She didn't have anyone. Having lived in Las Vegas before which, of course, is the desert, I would have just stayed at the house if there was absolutely nowhere else to go. Escaping into the desert was a pretty desperate move. In the midst of her desperate escape, Hagar thought that no one noticed her. So, like anyone who feels rejected, hurt or in need of immediate help, she began to cry in agony. And out of nowhere, an angel appeared, comforting her. This assured Hagar that God saw her, even when she thought she was alone. He promised to take care of her and her son. He kept His promise to bless them, despite the matter at hand. Though filled with drama, this story provides hope that God sees you, where you are and in whatever state you are. You may feel rejected like Hagar or maybe you're going through a time where you feel like God does not hear or see you. We are talking about your Father here. He provides comfort and He sees you. I dare you to call El ROI. Watch God fulfill promises that seemed impossible.

JEHOVAH RAPHA

When my baby brother, Emmanuel, was in middle school, he was diagnosed with a golf-ball sized tumor on the left portion of his cerebellum. Quite naturally, no one wants to hear this type of news, so as a family, we took it pretty badly. It was pretty devastating. Once doctors were certain that it was able to be removed, surgery was scheduled. The tumor was diagnosed on a Thursday and surgery was scheduled for the following Monday morning. While the doctors were scheduling surgery, my mom, being a woman of tremendous faith, was praying and asking God to perform a miracle for her baby. She was calling prayer warriors and intercessors to pray on Emmanuel's behalf. Over the course of the next five days, we were making the necessary arrangements to prepare for his recovery process and scheduling homeschooling for him. Never losing faith, my mom contacted the church she attended to request prayer. I even spoke to my pastor at the time and called my family, along with my brother, in for a special prayer the following Sunday after church. When he finished praying with the family, my pastor said, "Be sure to contact us with the good news." Full of faith, we said that we would.

Monday morning came and we were all going to Scottish Rite Children's Hospital in Atlanta to be with Manny during his surgery. My mom kept saying, "They are not going to cut my baby until we have another MRI." Surgery was scheduled for nine that morning, and doctors normally don't reschedule MRIs before surgery. My mom was persistent and her request was granted. We walked Manny into the room where he was to prep for surgery, but we were still waiting for them to call him for the MRI. Once we heard the call for the MRI, we headed up to the cafeteria to get food. We were starving because we had not eaten the night before. We wanted to support Manny because he could only have clear liquids for 12-14 hours before surgery. We finally made it to the cafeteria to eat, and before we could even start eating, we received a phone call saying to immediately return to surgery prep room where we'd left Manny. Not knowing what was going on, we left our food and our things and rushed right back to the operating floor. Getting off the elevator, we saw Manny and the surgeon walking towards us. Emmanuel was fully dressed and ready to go home.

"What's the problem?" my mom asked.

"Well, the problem is after the MRI, we could not trace the tumor that we were scheduled to remove this morning. Emmanuel is free to go home. You and your family can consider this a miracle," the surgeon said.

We filled the operating area with praise, tears of joy and thanksgiving to Jehovah Rapha, "God who heals". I even think my mom ran up the hallway as an outward expression of her gratefulness. Today, Emmanuel is 22 years old, and every year in August, we have a family dinner to honor Jehovah Rapha. We do this to always be mindful of His power and goodness.

You can live in optimal health because of Jehovah Rapha. When the name Jehovah Rapha is present, no other name related to sickness can exist. Sickness has different names, but the name of the Lord is greater. No other name stands in His presence. Diabetes, high blood pressure, HIV, arthritis, lymphoma, multiple myeloma, sickle cell, gout, anxiety, asthma, congestive heart failure are all names of diseases. None of them stand a chance when Jehovah Rapha is on assignment. Everything in its path is consumed. The stage of sickness, nor the manner of sickness matters. Tumors melt and cancer dries up. If you are currently dealing with any form of sickness, I join with you in agreement that Jehovah Rapha is making you whole. Not only does Jehovah Rapha heal physical illnesses, but He is the healer of broken hearts, broken spirits, broken emotions and relationships. I believe that if we get healed in our emotions, physical healing will be instantaneous. God alone provides the remedy for mankind's brokenness.

Scripture references: Jeremiah 30:17 Jeremiah 3:22, Isaiah 30:26, Isaiah 61:1, Psalm 103:3

JEHOVAH NISSI

Oh, say can you see by the dawn's early light
What so proudly we hailed at the twilight's last gleaming?
Whose broad stripes and bright stars thru the perilous fight,
O'er the ramparts we watched were so gallantly streaming?
And the rocket's red glare, the bombs bursting in air,
Gave proof through the night that our flag was still there.
Oh, say does that star-spangled banner yet wave
O'er the land of the free and the home of the brave?

The Star-Spangled Banner is the national anthem for the supposed United States of America. It was written to reflect the patriotic feelings of Francis Scott Key when he saw the enormous US flag flying over Fort Henry. The memorial that was made was the National Anthem, which followed the U.S. victory at the Battle of Baltimore, during the war of 1812.

Similarly, Jehovah Nissi was also the memorial for a battle won by the Israelites against the Amalekites in the 17th chapter of Exodus. Only this time, the banner was held by Moses on a hill as the battle was underway. On the hill is where the armies could see him and he could see them. As long as the banner was held up, the Israelites were winning. Moses was human, so quite naturally, his arms got tired and the banner fell. When the banner fell, the Amalekites had an advantage. So, Moses' brother, Aaron, and another Israelite named Hur held Moses' arms up as long as they could. Moses and his team realized that if the Israelites were to win this battle, they needed supernatural intervention because they were all tired and could no longer hold the banner. The Lord intervened. He held the banner until the Israelites won the battle. Moses built an altar there and called it, "the Lord is my Banner".

Moses and his team could not explain this win. The Israelites won by the power of God. The rod of Moses (the Banner) was held up in the same way that U.S. soldiers held up their flags in time of battle. They proudly fought under their flag—a flag that bore the emblem of the United States of America. Soldiers were happy to fight under their star-spangled banner. When you are engaged in warfare, remember that God is your banner. Hold His name up and you will be victorious. "Thanks be to God, who gives us the victory through our Lord Jesus Christ" (1 Corinthians 15:57).

Scripture reference: Exodus 17:15

JEHOVAH JIREH

God sets us up to assess whether or not we are committed and faithful to this journey with Him. He tests our giving to see if we are willing to give what He has blessed us with. He tests our love for one another. He also tests our integrity. There is one particular story in the Bible of a test—one that I am not sure I would have passed. It starts out with an outrageous command from God for Abraham to kill his son and sacrifice him as a burnt offering. Now, in the Bible days, these types of sacrifices were normal. A burnt offering in the Old Testament was usually an animal being killed and offered to God as a payment for sin. Shockingly, Abraham obeyed. He woke up the next morning and headed to Mount Moriah, the meeting place that God specified for him to kill Isaac. Isaac suspected that something strange was happening, because he did not see an animal. He said, "Dad, I see the fire and the wood, but where is the animal?" Ordinarily, Abraham would have an animal with him, so Isaac was likely piecing the story together in his mind.

"God Himself will provide a lamb for the burnt offering," Abraham told Isaac with faith as they continued up the mountain. At this point, I think Isaac is aware of what was going on and I am not sure why he was not going half crazy. When they finally got there, Abraham started preparing to kill his son. When he lifted the knife to kill Isaac, an angel suddenly appeared saying, "Abraham!!!" Relieved, Abraham immediately answered,

"YES GOD!!"

"Don't kill your son," said the angel. "You have proven that you honor and fear God since you were going to give him your only son."

Abraham looked up and saw a ram caught in the bush by his horns. He took the ram and offered it as a sacrifice to God in place of Isaac. Abraham called this placed JEHOVAH JIREH, meaning "The Lord Will Provide". I love this name of God even more now because I know what it means. Your provision might not come the way you expect. God will continue to provide as long as there is a need, and He will be right on time.

Scripture reference: Genesis 22:

El OLAM

There is a verse in the Bible that says, "Have you not known? Have you not heard? The everlasting God, the Lord the Creator of the ends of the earth, does not faint or grow weary or tired. His understanding is inscrutable." (Isaiah 40:28). This verse has helped me through some the most difficult times in my life, but honestly, I never knew there was a name dedicated to God's availability. I always thought that all good things had to come to an end. Good things should last forever. Especially God's goodness. It turns out that He does last forever. He created time so there is no end to Him. Similarly, He is described as the Ancient of Days because He existed before He created days. El Olam speaks to the unchanging and continuous essence of His goodness. God and His wonderful qualities last forever. Nothing about God grows tired! His power lasts forever. His mercy lasts forever. His love lasts forever. In church we say it like this, "God is good all the time, and all the time God is good." Church catchphrases are not my thing, but I love this one. This truth just so happens to be supported by a catch phrase.

The word *all* describes the quantity or extent of a particular thing. So, to the extent or the end of time, God is still good. Before days and time existed, God was, and when it ends, He will live on. He is El OLAM, the everlasting God.

"Before the mountains were born or you brought forth the earth and the world, from everlasting to everlasting you are God."
(Psalm 90:2)

Scripture references: Genesis 21:33 Jeremiah 31:3 Psalm 100:5

Names Hold Power

During my clubbing days, I loved going to different clubs with my friends. One thing I did not like was waiting in the long lines, especially when I knew all of the fun that was going on inside. Clubs would sometimes inflate their lines to draw curiosity. But, I became acquainted with people in high places. I knew club owners, promoters and other people who could get me and a few others in. Other times, my friends knew someone. We exchanged the favor. Bypassing the line was as simple as telling the crew at the door the name of the person who'd invited me. And just like that, we were in. That's because a name holds power.

For every great power that God has, there is a name. That name overrides anything that is contrary to that power. Jehovah Rapha overrides sickness. This is what makes it so difficult to adequately describe God and so easy to leave something out. Like God, each dimension of you has a purpose, whether you are a sister, mother, wife, daughter or friend. Remember what we discussed in the last chapter. At the sound of a name, some type of image is derived. You get to use your imagination, and now, you know the name above all names and He becomes a real force in your life. Your imagination will help you to create something great for every name. And YES, you are allowed to use your imagination. His names also reveal His identity. Since your identity is realized through God, it's only advantageous to learn of His names. Let the names of God take the place of any other influence that has tried to give you an identity.

There are two additional benefits that I noticed from knowing His names and qualities. In no particular order, one benefit was an enriched meditation time, in addition to a deeper understanding of His ways of functioning. Secondly, my worship life and reverence for God increased immensely when I learned His names. When we know who He is, we can worship Him from a deeper place. When I learned more about God, I had more to say to Him in conversations. And now, at the expression of His name, I find just what I need in the moment. As you worship God, you will find this to be your truth as well. Worship provokes His presence and His response.

It is not until we receive revelation about who God is that we know who we are because the names of God are more than just cute names to rattle off while in religious conversations. Every name should be taken seriously. The names of God were revealed to Abraham, David, Hagar, Moses, Gideon and others when there was a desperate need in their lives. God responded to their needs. We saw this as I told the various stories that memorialize the names. You have also witnessed His names too. I guarantee it. How many times have you needed money, gas, food, encouragement, or a bill paid, and did not know where it would come from? Somehow, your need was provided. Just the other day, Jehovah Jireh came through for me. I called to make a payment on a bill. I did not have the money for the bill, but I felt like Holy Spirit was leading me to call. When I inquired about making the payment, the representative said that the account had been paid in full. The name came to life when God actually became my Jehovah Jireh. No story can take the place of God actually showing up as the hero you read about. Others have experienced broken bones or other health maladies, some that have been deemed incurable by doctors, and some that were curable, but subject to time. These moments present the opportunity for Jehovah Rapha to show up and use His super healing power for His name's sake. It is His good pleasure to be all that we will ever need and more. This is why having a relationship with God is so important. Our relationship with God will not exceed our knowledge of who He is.

Without a personal relationship with God, we will continue to just read about Him, all the while, not knowing and experiencing Him.

When God makes a promise to you, His daughter, He plans to uphold His promise, just like He did for Hagar. God holds to His promises in order to uphold His name, because His name is on the line if there were ever a time that He did not deliver on His promise.

Knowledge of God is knowledge of self. As you begin to make the Lord your focus, use these names of God in your prayers and petitions to God. Pray to Him using the name that you need Him to be. Be careful not to wait until you need Him to pray. Your deeper focus on these great names of God will impact your connectivity with Him, and you will receive nuances about yourself and how closely connected you are to God. My hope is that God increases your hunger and thirst for Him so that He can reveal Himself to you in a new way.

CHAPTER 4

The Original Breath

"Every great masterpiece was made under the hand of a great artist"~ Apostle Bryan Meadows

"God said, Let Us [Father Son and Holy Spirit] make mankind in Our image, after our likeness, and let them have complete authority over the fish of the sea, the birds of the air, the [tame] beasts, and over all of the earth and over everything that creeps upon the earth. So God created man in His own image, in the image and likeness of God He created him; male and female, He created them."
Genesis 1:26-27 [AMP]

A key characteristic of our identities is that we are a complete replica of who God is. When He breathed His breath into us, He reproduced Himself. None of His other creations have His DNA or His breath. This speaks volumes of who you are and your value. The principle is that when God created you, He transferred Himself.

In the last chapter, we learned that Elohim distinctly communicates His desire for our lives to be fruitful. The fruitfulness of our lives will depend on our connectivity to His perfect plan and our decisions to choose His designated path. The implications of this text are so significant that fully exhausting the meaning of it would take years. However, in this chapter, the deeper meaning of God's original intent for your identity will be revealed. The concepts of God's plans for your life to dominate are achievable because you are a duplicate of Him. He would never put a demand on His creation that He does not equip us for. You have likely heard something similar before. I am not the only one that talks about identity. There is universal knowledge that we were built to make an impact in an area and God equipped us for the task.

Your uniqueness and identity are basically rooted in God's nature, and your ability to realize the unique set of qualities that you have has been provided. Your spirit is a true reflection of God, although your behavior may sometimes be the opposite. The way in which your mind conceptualizes and creates perspective about who God is, indeed provides insight into your life. Your mind also allows you to tap into your built-in potential to be great. That's why the mindset that you develop about who you are is critical.

God's intellect makes Him the all-wise and His will makes Him sovereign. We make decisions on a daily basis because He gave us this capability. As a matter of truth, our ability to reason and think comes from God. Every inherent capability is from God. We can all think in a different way because of God. Abstract or not, your ability to think at all comes from God. We can create because God is a creator; we can accomplish what sometimes looks impossible. We can dominate in our world because our Creator equipped us to have dominion. Simply put, man was created to have a superior, executive, dominating role in the Earth, to make the best use of the resources and to dominate it. As we say today, He created us to become bosses. We are to dominate in any area that God awards us stewardship in. The responsibility and mandate to have dominion is supported by how we have been created. Prior to God giving us this mandate, the world was fully created. "The firmaments were set in place and God separated the heavens from the Earth. Night was distinguished from the morning. God had established Kingdoms and each one had their own structure and laws." ~Apostle Bryan Meadows. God looked over His creation and called it good. Then God filled the space with people, places and things. God thought thoroughly about where He wanted you to live in the space that He created, even down to the street you grew up on.

The lack of understanding of the power of self-discovery is largely responsible for the failures, unhappiness, self-hatred, mental health disorders, and violence people experience in the world. It follows that the creative power of self-discovery has a vital role in mitigating negativity and cycles of depravity. A developed and strong sense of self is a great quality for creating your world well. Let's say you are someone who wants to change the world. You can, but not without changing yourself. Changing the world starts as an inside job.

Knowing who you are is an amazing gift with great benefits. Most people are inclined to think that they will be happy once they achieve a goal, get the mate they want, or buy their dream house. The truth is you will attract or create everything you want once you are happy. We attract what we don't want when our identities are not fully realized. Besides, if you can't think highly of yourself without a mate, money or a mansion, more inner work should be done. This truth begs the question, "Who are you without money, a mate or a mansion?"

A Father's Expectations

I think every father has expectations of his children. With that in mind, think about God, the Father. He told Adam and Eve to be fruitful and multiply. He didn't relegate being fruitful to just having children alone, because bearing children is not the only way to have a child. Some adopt, others find various ways to have children. Take my situation for example. I don't have children of my own, but I have worked in education for seven years and I have acquired mentees and those who I've been able to deeply impact and guide. God has given me stewardship over His children. I know several people who do the same in much greater capacities. They build empires around coaching, mentoring and developing others. These servants pour everything into the development of others. This concept is supported biblically.

This just means, replicate yourself in the world, on your job, in your church and in your family. John Maxwell calls this process succession-driven leadership. That means, once you have experienced success, the goal is to pay it forward. Teach someone everything you know. Don't learn things just to improve yourself, don't buy things to hoard them and don't go places without taking someone. Show people how to develop themselves into the individuals they want to be. Take someone through the process of metamorphosis and transformation.

God's Plan

A metamorphosis is a beautiful and relatively abrupt process that takes time. Butterflies begin their life cycle as eggs. When the egg hatches, we expect see a butterfly emerge, but that's not exactly how it happens. The next stage is the larva or the caterpillar. The job of the caterpillar is to eat the leaf that it was hatched onto. This second phase happens pretty quickly, so it's important that the caterpillar eats a lot and fast. After this, they endure two more phases before they actually become butterflies. To teach someone the process of anything you have done is multiplying yourself. I honestly don't know where I would be without my mentors and those who have allowed me to sit under their tutelage—those who have held my hand and guided me. God, being the genius that He is, had this all worked out. It was in His master plan. His desired result was for man to take over the Earth and bring it under control, and have dominion over the fish of the sea and over the birds of the air and over every living thing that moves on Earth. God's command to "subdue" the Earth means that you and I have the ability to be sitting on the throne of this kingdom called Earth, with everything under our authority, as we are led by His rule.

Taking a look at what it means to subdue the Earth, we gain an understanding of the concept of nurturing. We were created to be good stewards of the Earth and all of its vast resources. We learn this in science and in the Bible. The Earth or land is a resource in itself. If treated properly, it can be used to grow and harvest food for the masses. God created seeds that have the capability of the harvest until time comes to an end. These are what we call resources. Water is a resource. Animals are also resources. More specifically, goats, cows and chickens, and many farm-raised animals are useful to humans in more ways than one. These animals provide food for communities and create streams of income. Farmers learn to use land and animals through farming. We normally don't see the execution of the farming process because we are the end users on the supply chain. Even as end users, we play a part in the upkeep of the Lord's resources. Our cultivation of the Earth is important to God. Before the industrial revolution, the population depended on farming. People were healthy and happy. Unfortunately, farming could not keep up with the growing population.

We are leaders because we are made in the very image of a leader. Now, in order for us to have dominion as God commanded, a certain level of understanding must be embraced. We have a part of the bargain to uphold. With this position of authority comes responsibility. We must take the time to learn about all of God's handiwork, ourselves being first. In order to be a farmer, one would need to learn about agriculture. Agricultural laws must be learned to better understand the process of planting the seeds and harvest time. Once a farmer learns agricultural laws, there is no need to guess or worry about what will happen. Results are embedded into the laws. For instance, if a farmer plants an apple tree, he does not have to pray about the type of tree that will grow. The farmer will test various seeds in different soil types throughout the seasons. New farmers become agricultural experts over time.

Similarly, in order to have authority over an animal, one must study that animal in particular and become familiar with its kind. Thus far, the only humans that I have ever seen with proven power over animals are those who train animals, whether training the pet to perform or to simply become a pet. Either way, such skill takes commitment to understanding the animal. Learning how an animal behaves comes from studying the animal and spending time with the animal in its environment.

In the same way, we have been appointed to dominate in the marketplace. In order to become experts in specific fields, individuals would commit to being a continuous learners in specific areas. We all can have this type of authority. It is a mandate that God needs us to own. We have to become excited about and drawn to the process of learning. Everyone has this mandate. Some people don't have the mandate to be a farmer or animal trainer, but we ALL have the mandate to be good stewards over resources. Not everyone will dominate in the same area. Your ability to dominate is inside of you and what you will dominate is at your fingertips. He has already put it in your reach. What is it?

Your Creative Process

"And the Lord God formed man from the dust of the ground, and breathed into his nostrils the breath of life, then man became a living soul." Genesis 2:7 (KJV)

Your original DNA is an exact copy of your Creator; this is the same way we take the genetic traits of our parents. But the Creator's DNA was given to you even before your parents existed. For this reason in particular, it's impossible for you to be a mistake. You existed in the spiritual world before your mom and dad even met. Furthermore, YOUR creation required God's breath. Allow that to mean something personal to you! You are the largest asset to creation! Better yet, you have His nature because you have His breath or His identity. Think of your identity as your breath. It is an essential element of existence. The absence of breath is the absence of existence. Prior to God breathing the breath of life into Adam's nostrils, he was not living. He only had his physique, which further supports why looks and shapes are superficial. Nothing else mattered because Adam was not alive. He was just resting dead in the dirt. His spirit and his soul were lifeless. In that regard, identity is not defined by physical characteristics. Without the breath that God transferred into Adam, he would have been equal to the animals, but God saw to it that Adam should give the animals their name. This is another aspect of our nature that confirms why you did not evolve from a monkey. You were not created in the image of an animal. Would God, in His brilliance, even have it that way? NO! He thinks too much of you to make you equal to an animal. Adam solved a problem for God when he named the animals. You are also a problem-solver.

The BREATH

In the last chapter, we established that knowing only the basic meaning of words does not unlock the fullness of that word. In order to derive a deeper understanding of biblical texts and words, we must search out its meaning in depth. Definitions allow teachers, authors and speakers to drive their point home. How words are derived is a very interesting process. So, let's take a deeper look at the word *breath*. The word breath in the text is taken from the Hebrew word ruach. Ruach has several literal meanings such as life, intention, mind, air for breathing, strength, wind, breeze, spirit, courage, temperament, prosperity, power and purpose (Strong's Concordance, 7307). While this list displays the literal meanings of ruach, it represents and symbolizes the identity that God gave to us when He breathed into Adam's nostrils. All because of the ruach, you have God's courage, power boldness, mind, wisdom, prosperity and every perfect gift from Him. This took place long before you were created in your mother's womb. The transfer of identity from God to man was all in the breath. Alone, this confirms why there is an insurmountable level of power connected to our breath. Therefore, everything that God IS has been transferred into you. Accordingly, you can think, act, be creative, exude power, have purpose, have wisdom, love and prosper like God. We also have God's supernatural strength. One of the aspects of our identities is not only knowing who we are, but knowing what we have access to as His creation.

Although God breathed one breath into Adam's nostrils, His breath revealed His brilliance as each of us are still unique in our existence. You still have to think of yourself as an individual and take the transference personally. All humans have God's breath, but none of us were made to do the same thing. One breath was split many different ways to create you and me and generations unborn. Take a moment to thank God for thinking enough of you to give you His identity. You don't have to accept the world's identity when God has given you His. Elohim put His breath in us and He is the air we breathe. How cool is that! STOP for a moment. Close your eyes and take a deep breath in. Let it out. Any way you look at it, God gave you that breath.

The INTENTION

Anything that is not done intentionally is left to chance. YOU were not left to chance because God was intentional about your creation. God was thinking about the generations unborn that would be produced from you. God wanted to create someone who He could get the most use out of to bring Him glory. For this reason, no one should be able to compartmentalize you or limit your skills to one function or dimension. The same way that God is multidimensional, so are you. He is a healer, He is all-powerful, eternal, holy, omniscient, and so much more. Most importantly, He is God. Don't be tricked into believing that God has no need of you. Your existence proves that He does. That's called intention. Remember, God created the Garden (need) first, and then He created Adam as a fulfillment to that need. Adam's job was to cultivate the land, till the ground and work. After this, He created the woman to help the man. However, women are not limited to our assignment as help-meets. Women create wealth, speak out for the destitute, save lives, build our homes, break records, help the poor, protect our families, and so much more. We meet needs and solve problems. Our job is to understand what God created us to do. On a broader scale, He wants us to be His hands, mouth and feet on the Earth. God had an eternal plan, and we are a part of it. Not to mention, He has a superpower to predict the end from the beginning. He indulges Himself by what He does through us. He often gives us desires that mirror His desires for our lives. This is what the scripture means when it says, "He will give you the desires of your heart."

God's MIND

God's mind is the epitome of creativity. Just read the first chapter of the Bible. Better yet, just take a look around. Everything you see, living and nonliving, is evidence of His work. "The skies display God's craftsmanship" (Psalm 19:1). The mind of God is a supernatural, creative force that allows Him to be all-wise, all-knowing and all-powerful at the same time. His desire was to impart His very same mind into you. And He did. Do you realize how much power lies in your mind? I don't believe that there is anything more powerful. Every function of your brain and your mind is a reflection of God's mind.

The mind is the place where thoughts and ideas are formed. With your mind, you understand who you are. With your mind, potential is developed. It's also where intellectual strength is formed. You are able to develop the fortitude needed to stay the course when life gets rough in your mind. Attitude is developed in the mind; peace is cultivated in the mind. Your life is hinged on your state of mind. I've even heard it expressed this way, mental health is total health. The ability to focus, work a job, raise children, decide, mediate, answer tough questions, think and speak simultaneously comes from the power of your mind. Your mind can take you to a place that you have only dreamed of going. That's the power of your mind. The power of your mind reflects the brilliance of God's mind.

This is why your mind should not be left to flow. You have a brilliant mind. But, it will go anywhere if you allow it. "Your mind is always discovering and defining what it perceives" ~Dr. Caroline Leaf. The greatest aspect about your mind is that you control it. If your mind has been programmed to think negatively, you have the power to change it. It's in your mind that battles are first won. I believe that once there is an awareness of the power of the mind, we will be able to better manage our mental environments. "What goes on in our mind should be what we choose rather than what we are subjected to" ~Dr. Caroline Leaf.

Thoughts produce words. Words are real forces that create worlds, whether the one we live in together or your individual world. Additionally, thoughts activate emotions and are designed to help us get an understanding. Our emotions and our minds are linked; they work together, but are not the same. You can decide how you feel by using the power of your mind. Your mind always has the upper hand. We say it this way. Mind over matter. RIGHT!!

God's POWER

Have you ever had more to do in one day than the time would allow? Or have you ever made it through a difficult situation that you thought would leave you broken down? To date, I'm amazed as to how I've come out on the winning side. What I know is that on my own, I would have thrown in the towel. But, in my weakness, God provides strength. How does one find the desire to live every day after an incurable diagnosis? I believe that God's power is at work within them, even without being acknowledged.

God's power alone jerks tears from men that would never cry in public. It finds its way into broken hearts and wounded souls. God's power saves people that were lost, heals those who may have been sick and revives those who were dead. The same power helps us perform our everyday functions. We find power in prayer, meditation, the study of God's Word and other spiritual disciplines. God's Spirit is the spirit of power. "For God, has not given us the spirit of fear, but of power and of love and of calm and well balanced mind and discipline and self control." (II Timothy 1:7, AMP) With God's power, nothing can harm us, even on our weakest day of the week. I don't know of anything that can cut through this type of power.

God's purpose, power and passion were revealed when He created you. Therefore, you are God's complete responsibility. The complexities that surround your creation magnify the power of His intention. His intention was intertwined in His plan to prosper, keep and guide you to your best life. Living your best life is a powerful way to live, but it will demand the best you to be present. So, as we close this chapter, I want to invite you on a spiritual journey to increase the awareness of your breath by engaging in constant prayer, conversation, meditation and the study of His Word. You will discover what it takes to live in God's intention for your life. "If you wait to until you get in trouble to engage with God, then I am afraid that you are already in trouble." ~unknown

CHAPTER 5

Choked

"The thief cometh not, but for to steal, kill, and to destroy…"
John 10:10

"If we don't act now to safeguard our privacy, we could all become victims of identity theft." Bill Nelson

Like most people, I have swallowed water down my windpipe which, of course, is the "wrong pipe." You would likely agree this is the most unpleasant feeling of helplessness ever. Your throat closes up and you literally can't breathe. You can exhale by coughing uncontrollably, but that's only one part of breathing. The instinct to inhale is NOT HAPPENING! Your eyes start to water and your chest feels compressed. The external activity of choking is a horrible feeling because while choking, you are panicking inside as you are trying to regain control of your breath, all the while creating a cycle of internal and external obstruction. Your life is flashing before your eyes and seconds can feel like an eternity. At the moment, recovery from the choking episode seems out of reach. That is because choking is sometimes caused by conditions that we have less control over, hindering our ability to stop it from happening. In the same way that choking on a liquid threatens physical breathing, life's challenges have the tendency to pose a threat on our identities, This can affect our qualities of life.

Have you read the story of Daniel? He was the boy who had been given the opportunity to become rich if he denied God. Well, he became rich but without ever negotiating his beliefs. Daniel and all of his friends were taken to a foreign land at a very young age. They were taken far away from everything that they knew, which included their families and their social networks. They were taken to a place called Babylon. The Babylonian's intentions were to brainwash them into adopting the Babylonian lifestyle. This was a lifestyle contrary to everything they knew. This was just like slavery. The goal was to change their thinking, their work style, and their views. Originally, they knew God well, but the Babylonians wanted their lives subjected to the values imposed on them. They tried to change their names and give them new identities. Their old names reflected their original relationship with God, but the new names pointed to false gods. The Babylonians did anything to cause Daniel and his friends to become futile and forget about God and their identity, but, Daniel and his friends were strong. The attempt to disconnect them from their roots was unsuccessful as they refused the Babylonian culture. They remained faithful to God. From rejecting rich food to praying after being told not to, they did not bend. Daniel showed great integrity and Godly character. In doing so, he earned the respect of the same king that wanted to kill him. Daniel's devotion to his God brought attention to God. The evil king praised and honored Daniel's God, as the Most High. God rewarded Daniel's faithfulness.

The story of Daniel is a constant encouragement as the media becomes stronger in its influence on this media-controlled generation. This summary of Daniel's story is a snapshot of how the world's system wants to stamp a false identity on us. It wants to choke the breath of our souls until we panic and conform to the disgraceful conditions of our society. We are heavily inundated with messages as the world tries to tell us who we are, where we should live, how we should spend our money, what to drive, how and who we should date. They (systems) try to trivialize the greatness and purpose of God, as well as His omniscience, all for the purpose of killing our relationship with God, stealing our vitality and destroying our existences. Our very intentions are violated by the enemy's pursuit of our identities. This includes all of the qualities that are embedded into who we became when God breathed into Adam. But, just like Daniel, we have to be bold and decide to stand our ground. We have to decide not to conform to the systems of this world. This point becomes piercingly clear to me as I make strides to understand what has caused the plight of our society and what caused the plight in my own life. It's important that we understand that God created us from Himself to be the answer to the problems that the world is experiencing. In essence, the reason I highlighted so extensively who God is in the prior chapter is partly to ensure that you see a picture of who you are so clearly that other images are obliterated. You are who you are because God is inside of you and you've decided to embrace Him. So, the thief expresses his disapproval with you by setting up ways to keep you living under the influence of ignorance. If we are being honest, many of us have sided with the media and accepted the fairy tale identities that it has placed on us.

The Enemy At Work

One factor that comes with being chosen by God is that you become vehemently targeted by the devil. Remember, he is a thief and his plan is to destroy the plans that God has designed even before you were conceived. So, the common attack that the enemy will launch against you targets your identity and your awareness of your identity. He is not interested in your car, house, figure, or anything superficial. Tangible items represent the lowest part of you and pose no threat to him. The realization of your identity threatens his tactics against your life. The enemy knows, sometimes better than most of us, that with self-discovery comes power over every attack, purpose, authority, favor, confidence, wisdom, strategy, abundance, dominion and a great life. Remember, you were born with all of this. It's your birthright to possess each as a stamp of your identity. He knows that a concealed identity makes a person more vulnerable to an attack. He also knows that victory is inevitable when we know what we have access to as God's children. For this reason, he works diligently to deceive us into being fearful, depressed, having low self-esteem, vacillating back and forth between emotions and questioning whether or not we were made in God's image. Our lives, having varying degrees of difficulties and responses, create barriers for believing that we have indeed been created in an incorruptible way. The enemy will use our disbelief against us to create more identity confusion. That is, so we define ourselves based on a inaccurate views of who we are and forfeit the opportunity to become who God created us to become.

But this did not start with our individual experiences as some may think. Our encounters with the enemy are not unique. We say, "No one understands what I'm going through." With all the people on this Earth, do you really think that NOBODY understands you? Well, guess what? Satan tested Jesus first. And Jesus gives us a special note in 1 Corinthians 10:13. He says, "No temptation has overtaken or enticed you that is not common to the human experience nor is any temptation unusual or beyond human resistance." In other words, there is nothing that we will experience in this world that Jesus did not have to deal with first, which means that He knows how to lead you to victory. Satan knows exactly when and with what tactic he will use to attack you. He has peered into your future and studied your life play by play. He tries to interfere with your wins just like he did to Jesus. In Luke 4, the devil challenged Jesus in three areas.

1. His heritage. He said "If you are the son of God you should turn this stone into a loaf of bread." Jesus said, "It is written a person can't live by bread alone." What Jesus is saying is, I know who I am and what I have to offer. I am the Bread of Life, and natural bread is not enough for sustenance anyway. My Word is what you will need to live.
2. His omnipotence. Satan said, "I will give you all power and authority and excellence, preeminence dignity and prosperity of these nations if you worship me." Jesus replied, "It is written, worship the Lord your God, and serve only the Lord." He tried to offer Jesus something that He already owned and that is EVERYTHING! How can you give Jesus what He already has?
3. His divinity. Satan told Jesus, "If you are the Son of God, you should jump down from here. For, it is written God

will command the angels for you and will guard and watch over you closely. And also, in order that you do not hit your foot against a stone, the angels will support you by the hand." So, he was telling Jesus to jump from the mountain and prove that He had angels designated to save His life. Jesus answered again, "It has been written, you shouldn't test the Lord your God." Jesus was saying, devil, you must be confused about who I Am. Since you are, maybe you should go ask around. Jesus is not to be played with.

All of Satan's challenges were deceitful attempts to separate Jesus from the truth. Satan is clever and bold. Didn't he know that Jesus is the Truth? These are not my words; the Bible tells us that He is. There he was trying to tempt Jesus who is full of supernatural power. He was trying to wear down Jesus' will, bringing to question His own power and identity.

He fights us with the same intensity. I am sure this comes as no surprise, as you have been tempted as well. Truthfully, he will never be able to destroy God's plans, but he does know how to use situations to choke us. This is to keep us from seeing God's plans. Choking creates a frantic state that stops a person in their tracks. A person choking is not able to use their mind fully to charge ahead aggressively in pursuit of purpose. No one is exempt from the enemy's tactics. As someone passionate about my life's work, my responsibility is to help you use the understanding of who you are to dribble, dribble and spin past the attack of the enemy just like Allen Iverson would do to his opponents during a basketball game. Then, he would charge to his destination—the goal for two-points. You already have the tools. All I can do is help you to unearth what you have not yet tapped into. As you discover your identity, the personal issues that we have all faced at some point will be simple to overcome. These issues include low self-esteem, the need for validation, comparison, shame, guilt, dishonesty, self-limiting beliefs, anger, dependency, anxiety, fear, depression and lack of confidence.

Becoming privy to the Satan's tactics allow you to prepare and stand on guard when the next one comes. You can pass the test without question by seeing yourself the way God sees you.

As you live day-to-day, you will become aware of the ways in which life will attack your identity. The enemy will strategize an attack with your name on it. It will meet you where you are heading. Every test will come as scheduled (if it's not interrupted). You have to remember that the enemy we are facing is wise (not as wise as God). He knows who you are and the treasures that you have. He also knows your weaknesses and proclivities. His attacks are sometimes subtle, but grow in intensity with repetition. You saw this when he tempted Jesus. Every temptation was more enticing than the last. I want you to understand the spiritual war underway concerning your identity. Remember, your enemy is unable to create, so his purpose is to destroy, steal and conceal what God's purpose is for your life. He will use almost anything to do it.

Identity Theft

In 2004, a man was found beaten and left for dead behind a Burger King in South Georgia. When found, his body was covered in red marks, seemingly ant bites. He was naked and had no identification available. The woman who found him called the police and immediately rushed him to the hospital. Upon being admitted, he was found to be in stable condition, but he suffered from Premium or what doctors are calling Retrograde Amnesia. He could not remember any aspect of his identity; this was possibly the result of trauma to his head. Because he did not know his birth name, the hospital nicknamed him Benjamin Kyle. He had no recollection of any past, family members, childhood memories, siblings, old addresses or anything. He described himself as a ghost because he was legally nonexistent. For 11 years, he went through strenuous procedures designed to help him recall any type of event from his past, but to no avail. This story received national prominence when Kyle was featured on the Dr. Phil Show and several different organizations committed to helping him attempt to regain his identity. It was strange that no one came looking for him, even after he was featured on a nationally syndicated show. He could not get an identification card, a job or go to the bank. This went on for over 11 years until he was able to give doctors a date. Doctors assumed that this date was his birthday. Benjamin Kyle was able to obtain a State of Florida Identification Card. The documentary begins, "Hello, my name is Benjamin Kyle. You don't know who I am and, quite frankly, neither do I."

Here, we have a man who is completely void of his natural identity. Electronic fingerprinting methods, as well as the old ink method did not allow the FBI to locate his identity in any database. DNA tests led researchers nowhere. With no family to lean on for support, no resources and no one looking for him, Benjamin Kyle was passed from hospital to hospital in Savannah, Georgia until a woman allowed him to move in with her. This was a pretty desperate situation to be in, especially since Mr. Kyle's well-being was at the mercy of strangers—the people who were responsible for his care. The one fact that reverberated with me was that he had to be subjected to the name people gave him.

While this story depicts the natural identity being taken from the innocent, we can agree that the goal of the enemy is to conceal our spiritual identity, which affects every other part of our being, consequently causing our lives to spin out of control in a downward spiral into chaos. Similar to the effect of the natural identity being stolen, when this happens, we are unable to control how we are addressed. If we don't know who we are, in turn, no one else will. The lack of identity is detrimental to the overall well-being of a person because it does not allow an individual to possess the assertion, maturity or knowledge needed to provide the truth and demand respect. Add to that the inability to make decisions that affect one's day-to-day well-being.

With the unnecessary brutality, domestic violence, gang violence, credit card thefts, school shootings and drug rings, very few would dispute that something is desperately wrong in the world we live in. These outward demonstrations of violence are a reflection of inner dis-ease. People are shooting others for senseless reasons. There are people who are being forced to endure the inconceivable, as they are in the hands of wicked people. Mentally disturbed men sexually exploit hundreds of adolescent girls in Atlanta alone. Proliferating crime exists right under our noses. Every senseless act can be traced back to lack of self-discovery. Lack of identity awareness (interchangeable with self-discovery) is at the root of all of the aforementioned trauma.

What's Wrong?

What is the root cause of any of this? To maintain the book's theme, we will just ask "What is it that chokes the breath out of us?" or "What conceals our identities?" Overall, we have not fully nurtured the awesome power and treasure that we have within us. As a result, we sabotage our happiness, health and success. Additionally we don't create a powerful and attractive version of ourselves. That's the short answer.

We all would love to think that we are without issues or that someone is to blame for the issues that we have. Very few people take full responsibility of the path their lives have taken. Excuses and blame trump the responsibility. For so long, I hid the real path that my life had taken. Outwardly, I was successful, but that meant nothing because my soul was anemic and in need of a transformation. "I'm good." I would say this to mask my truth as if there is a charge for admitting that I needed help or that something was wrong. But, I didn't want to look weak or as if I didn't have it together. Rather than expose my desperate state of need and work towards a possible improvement, the most convenient thing to do was act like I had it all together. That's what everyone does, right? I was one of those people who was seen as strong. Really, I just knew how to fake so well that it looked like a strength. This really worsens the situation, creating inner chaos which will manifest publically at some point. These situations, when unaddressed, almost never end well. On the news, we see it as a mass shooting, suicide, domestic violence, and various forms of abuse or problems. YES! I could have been a murderer or a victim of suicide. My pain was deep and I refused to deal with it. I gave into the stigma, putting too much value into what people would think.

The reason for the world's plight is that we have not dealt with our own personal issues or realized our greatness. We disregard them and keep saying, "I'm good." There are more millionaires in this society than the world has ever seen, but overall, we are hopeless. People are working their dream jobs and hopeless; they are driving their dream cars and hopeless. People are great at their jobs, but struggle to keep themselves happy. That's because no type of money or achievement can provide the air we need to live. I know it sounds so obvious and cliché to say that money can't buy happiness. Nonetheless, this statement is worth saying again and again from the mountaintops. When we are given the opportunity to live well or fake like we are, we choose the latter out of convenience. I made brokenness look blessed. I dressed up my pain in a designer outfit and I was living life scandalously, not taking care of my soul. I allowed myself to be swayed by stigma and bullied by misrepresentations of happiness. Take my situation and add it to the millions of people who are experiencing astronomical devastation without counseling and you get the tragic state of our world. The world is in need of healing because individuals are in need of healing.

Stigma won't allow people to make conscious decisions to make self-care a priority. We think it highlights weakness. Most of us don't truly understand the meaning of weakness. A weakness is only bad if it's not used as a means to expose strength. And weakness definitely does not mean inability or disability. But, we have learned how to fake it so that we can look good in the eyes of others who are as good at faking it. This is when weakness becomes dysfunction.

I believe this is why interviewers ask their applicants, "Tell me about your weakness." The goal is to see how we are able to dig ourselves out of strenuous situations, plus, it shows that we indeed have strengths. It shows that no two people think the same way. We are amazingly unique. It also reveals the awareness of our strengths and weaknesses, thus, proving that we are able to accomplish our goals, despite our frailties. I believe that a hidden weakness is more noticeable, especially when there is a tendency to compensate for lack. Knowing where there is room for improvement presents the opportunity to master a skill, to grow and to develop new strengths.

On the other hand, weakness could cause others to underestimate us. Being underestimated has an advantage. Mattie James said it this way, “When people are not looking at you as you grow, there is more room to make errors, push through the growing pains and get better without a bunch of eyes on you.” I have taken full advantage of this concept.

Identity Crisis

What I have found is that lack of self-discovery is at the core of most personal issues. Namely, lack of forgiveness, jealousy, relational issues, depression, low self-esteem, fear, people-pleasing, guilt, self-rejection, lack of boundaries, self-sabotage and looking for love in the wrong places, amongst hundreds of others. These are the symptoms of an identity crisis. An identity crisis is any situation that prohibits an individual from operating based on the original intent for their existence. It stops us from advancing in every area of our lives. When any of these symptoms exist in the life of a person, the chances of being unscathed by life's obstacles are rare. A symptom is not what’s wrong, it’s a signal that lets the human brain know that something IS wrong. For example, attention-seeking is a symptom of a deeper issue, such as lack of self-acceptance.

Have you ever had a headache or a cold, and the only thing you did was fight the symptoms by taking a pill for the pain or the cough, rather than fighting the germ that caused it? I GET IT! Sometimes, immediate relief is a miracle in itself when fighting excruciating pain, but immediate relief could also mean forfeiting the long-term cure. Medicine is available to alleviate almost all symptoms. However, side effects from medicine often add to the problem and create vicious cycles or worsening symptoms.

A fever is an indication that there is an infection somewhere in the body. Similarly, pain could be symptomatic of a broken bone. Although I have only experienced a sprain, I can only imagine that a broken bone is far more painful. There are not enough painkillers in the world and no amount of tiger balm could heal the fracture. A different type of treatment must be administered. Actually, various types of treatment may be necessary to remedy pain and reach long-term healing. For instance, when I was going for the treatment of depression and anxiety, I integrated cognitive behavioral therapy with my faith, daily confessions, meditation, breathing exercises, mindfulness, working out, and self-discovery. Depression and anxiety were symptoms of several deeper problems. So rather than try to remedy a symptom, we have to think beyond the symptom and trace each problem back to its root. Using this model, we can better understand the difference between treating symptoms and curing the condition. This is done in business, medicine, and should also be done in life.

At the start of this book, I showed your original position in the Earth and your position of dominion. When Adam and Eve disobeyed God in the garden, a deal was made with the devil. This agreement made his attacks against us fair game. He also gained insight into our identities, and we have been fighting to regain our original position ever since. Looking at where we started up until now, automatically begs the question, "If we were created by God to live powerful lives, have dominion and bear His nature, what is it that's powerful enough to remove us from such a place? What attacks our sustenance and quality of life?"

The short answer is, your enemy is working overtime to make sure you never find out your gifts or your purpose for being alive. Your discovery will destroy his pursuit against you. With such profound knowledge, you will have enough strength to blow his kingdom down.

"Lest Satan should get an advantage of us; for we are not ignorant of his devices." II Corinthians 2:11
Learning his tactics will strengthen your plan of attack. Here is what he tries to use against you.
"RELIGION"

Let's face it!! Some of us have not been taught how to integrate our faith into everyday life. I am one who lived in this form of bondage most of my Christian life because of religion. Not religion as in the system of faith, worship or belief in a higher power. I am speaking of religion, meaning, control, loyalty to certain concepts, traditions and practices without an understanding of its principles. We have mastered an outward form of religion, but it's not enforced by a relationship with the very emblem of the faith, Jesus Christ, or the power of His counterpart, the Holy Spirit. Remember Adam's body without the spirit was dead. The same is true for religion.

Collectively, as humans we have an undeniable tendency to be critical of anything that does not resemble what we are familiar with. Consequently, it has been said that Sunday morning is one of the most segregated days of the week. You can only imagine what is happening everywhere else if separation is the face of the religious sector. Sometimes, we don't hold ourselves accountable for the same rules we want others to adhere to. We criticize people for having our same secret sin. We hold man-made dogmatic systems as the standard, and we are loyal to these systems, even though they have proven to be invalid and pointless. Our focus has shifted to things that apparently have nothing to do with the Word of God or what really makes people who they are. So, we dress people up and give them a list of rules that they are forbidden to break, all the while, trying to convince them to behave a certain way. We watch as their identities are concealed by long skirts, dry faces and an oppressive list of religious dogma. This can end when we individually endeavor to have a personal relationship with Jesus and allow His Holy Spirit to lead us into truth.

REJECTION

I don't think there is anyone who has ever lived who has not experienced rejection. We have all been told no or been denied of something. We meet rejection from every angle. Unfortunately, rejection impacts our lives leaving deep wounds. Think about those wounds that cut to the white part of your flesh, leaving a scar.

Simply put, rejection is the feeling of being unwanted, to be put out, told no, left out. Like the rest of us, a person who deals with rejection often wants to belong. However, after a person marries the idea that they are rejected and unwanted, they will live in a world of self-sabotage. Consequently, they reject any type of care that is genuinely available to them. To compensate for rejection, some people do things that will make them feel more desirable and accepted. Some people become perfectionists, thinking they can make up for their being rejected by producing perfect work. Others overproduce, thinking that work on any level will cause them to be accepted.

When I was in grade school, kids that were not well-known were called rejects. At the time, I did not think that the idea of being rejected would potentially ruin a person's life. For us, reject just meant "outcast".

There are many ways to experience rejection. Some experience abandonment, molestation, victimization, birth defects, wrongful termination, mistreatment, or just being told NO. These are only a few. Some of these experiences happen at an early age and changes how we see ourselves. Being molested as a child opened a door in my life for rejection to enter. Also, not growing up with my biological father had a negative effect on my identity. Because I did not treat the wound, other areas of my life became infected. I did not acknowledge the emotions that arose from the adverse experiences and they emerged again more aggressively. I became a pretty unhealthy adult. I craved the approval of men to the point of allowing mistreatment in order to feel loved. I was afraid of any type of real intimacy. When a man tried to come in, I often slammed the door . I did not like the thought of being left again. I wanted a real relationship, but developing a healthy relationship with a man seemed futile. I did not know how to deal with being rejected. Trying to sweep the emotions under the rug only made a big mess. This is unhealthy because what we don't face will turn around and bite us on the behind. People didn't notice my shame because I was good at covering up anything that I was not proud of. I knew exactly what to do to make myself likable to others.

Our susceptibility to rejection is because we are wired to naturally want acceptance. The desire to be accepted is so strong that we will do desperate things to satisfy the desire. We shrink back, play dumb, say yes, and buy things we don't like. I agreed with people just to be liked. I went places because I did not want to be left out. The effects of rejection are layered with a disadvantage.

OPINIONS OF OTHERS

We all have opinions that we can offer based on experience and bias. So, you don't have to search long or hard to find someone offering an opinion. Some people are skilled at giving their opinions to mold others into what they want them to be. People bondage is so common today because we are a generation that values the opinions of others over our own core values and convictions. The opinions of others have become our source of living and have come from individuals who are less positive or less effective than we are. Sometimes, we don't trust our own judgment because life's obstacles have a way of making us forget our strengths and lose awareness of our competence. Furthermore, when we begin to question what we know to be true based on an opinion is when the problem arises.

Obviously, we all will need to seek counsel from professionals and qualified individuals at the right time. Even then, counselors have the role of helping clients dig deeply to find their own answers, because you have the answers even in the midst of turmoil. You have been given authority, and you give this authority away when you neglect to utilize it. You have been created to solve problems; starting with your own. It's important that you listen to those inner promptings that some call the "gut." I believe it's the Holy Spirit. Ignoring it weakens your sensitivity to it, creating dependency on advice from other people. God's wisdom is available to you. His wisdom trumps any advice or opinions from others. His wisdom protects and guides us to abundant lives.

FADS

Fads draw our attention to do what is trending, when we can be setting the trend and doing whatever we choose. We imitate one another in the dominant hairstyles and haircuts that we choose to wear and even in games or gadgets we buy. When I was in high school, the girls wore what we called Waterfalls with a flip. In my mom's day, they wore Bobs or asymmetrical cuts. Today, hair extensions and being natural are the biggest hair fads.

All fads are not negative, but I think the propensity to imitate is deeply rooted in rejection and in upbringing.

Now fads are a prevalent part of popular culture. It's easier and more acceptable to just do what everyone else does. Right? Some professionals call this herding. Have you ever seen how sheep gather and follow each other in a herd? When I lived in Texas, I had the opportunity to attend a few of the Rodeo Livestock shows. I sat in awe watching how the sheep always ended up together. The lost one or two always made their way back to the herd after its part in the show was done. I was so shocked by the sheep's instincts that I missed most of the show. Humans sometimes display the same patterns, never considering that many tasks in life will require an individual effort. I get it. We all have to follow before we lead, but while following, we still have individual personalities, goals and purposes that can't be achieved with the "pop culture" mentality.

What I have noticed about some of these FADS is that they don't allow us to be certain or proud of who we are. They pressure us to conform, and the payoff is usually unfavorable. And many times, we partake in fads of which we do not know the origin. We do it JUST because others are doing it. #trending

One fad that I utterly HATE with every fiber of my being is a modern-day trend of people calling each other BITCH. Apostle Kim Daniels says, "This is a name used to curse women. When this is spoken over a woman, it is meant to release immorality, lewdness, spiteful vengeance and overbearing domination. This spirit manifests itself perfectly through homosexual men who open themselves and take pride in being called a bitch" (The Demon Dictionary, p. 8-9). As you can see, it's not a word that is reflective of a person who is made in the image of God. That's all of us. The pressures to confirm are strong because it seems as if everybody is saying it. Celebrities say it. Men say it, women say it, the rich say it, the poor say it, adults say it and the kids say it.

One day, as I was sitting at my desk, I heard one of my kindergarten students use this word to talk to a classmate. I was outraged as I rushed over to the student. I wanted to snatch her up out of her seat and fuss at her for using such foul word. However, I know at such an impressionable age, children often say what they hear. So, I asked her, "Who did you hear say this word?" I was mortified when she replied, "My big sister and my mom call me that." The only thing I could think to do in that moment was console her and affirm who she REALLY is. I could not punish her for telling me such a devastating truth. I did not want to believe what my ears had just heard. This paradigm has to change.

CHALLENGE: I want to stop right here and personally challenge you to stop using this word and also stop allowing people to refer to you with this word. Demand that people respect themselves and your space. You don't have to take it. Furthermore, if you don't address the problem, you become a part of it. Open your mouth and express your disapproval. People won't stop unless you say, "Don't call me that." And challenge them also to stop saying it altogether. In order to stop a habit, you must replace the habit. So, chose another word like woman, daughter, queen or something positive. BE CREATIVE!

The pressure is real. And it's hard to practice individuality when the trends look so cool. I found it difficult to be the only one not doing what's popular. But, being an individual is more important than doing what is popular. When someone refers to himself or herself in such a derogatory way, it's apparent that they have adopted a belief that they are this word. "When someone has believed that something is true, whether it is or not, they act like it."~Dr. Robert Anthony. The concept that words have power is universal knowledge. We have the power to change the dynamics of our lives with words. Every day, we must confess what we want to manifest. This works both ways. We can't make negative confessions, even in casual conversations and allow ourselves to think those words aren't creating. "Both death and life are in the power of our tongues" (Proverbs 18:21). Either way, whether you are saying your confessions in the morning before you start your day or having a conversation, words create real things. Thinking does the same. In fact, thoughts become words ultimately. Your words create your world. The brain and the spiritual realm responds to thoughts and words as commands. As a result, those who call themselves derogatory names often subconsciously do things like search for facts that support what they believe. They behave like, look like and even attract what they have been confessing. What do you believe about yourself? Whatever it is has now become your identity. Everything that you attract in your world is based on what you believe.

CONDEMNATION

Have you ever been shocked that even after being saved, you still sinned? Don't be! I grew up in a Christian home and I felt like being born again would make me perfect. It did not! I still messed up, failed and made mistakes. One of the mistakes that literally shook me to my core was losing my virginity before marriage. Seriously, I thought my life was over. That's because of the major emphasis placed on being a virgin until marriage. I thought abstaining would make me pure. That's what we are taught. But the problem arises when we don't understand why this principle is important. I know! That's what God wants, but we make it seem like sexual purity is the only requirement of God, when He requires purity of heart, mind and deed. He wants our motives to be pure. So, I felt like a fraud because I was professing to be a Christian. I was not married and no longer a virgin. I carried the condemnation of my broken promise. I thought my relationship with God was ruined. I literally stopped eating and became depressed and ashamed. I felt like God had it out for me because of my mistake. If you are reading this book and you feel like me, understand that Jesus died so that you do not have to carry around that feeling of condemnation. Remaining sexually pure requires more than just establishing that, "God wants me to abstain from sex until marriage." In these days, we want to know why and it's okay to ask God, "Why?" Once we understand why, we become empowered. God wants our memories as well as our relationships to be protected. He also wants us to build intimacy with a person. Intimacy is so much better than sex. When we understand this and get revelation from God for our lives individually, we see abstinence as a gift rather than a curse. It really takes the supernatural help of the Holy Spirit AND clear boundaries to remain a virgin.

After it happened, I did not know how to approach God. After all, sex before marriage is the end of the world. At least that's what condemnation says. I became brutally judgmental of myself. The good news is God does not hold our sins over our heads. Spiritual leaders made me feel like he would be eternally mad. He was not mad at all. He just wants us to talk to Him like a daughter would talk to her father. I gained strength by simply going to Him honestly and asking for forgiveness and help in order to move on from the mistake. Once I confessed to the Lord, I no longer had to be held captive by what I'd done wrong or sentence myself to a life of punishment. Your responsibility is to confess it to God. After this, ask for forgiveness and help to live sexually pure. God wants to help you change your mind and understand that He is not permit condemnation. He has already taken your sins and He will not remind you of them. A decade later, I finally accepted His forgiveness. The question is, why do we still feel guilty after we have asked for forgiveness? The simple answer is that the devil uses condemnation as a tactic to keep us in a place of ignorance. Also, after being forgiven, we must ask God for understanding and truth. The devil will do anything to destroy our relationship with our Father. This way, we will not live the fulfilled lives that God has planned for us. He knows that if we are regretful and living with the guilt of our past lives, the plans that God has for our lives will become useless.

MEDIA

We barely have to turn on our televisions anymore before we are inundated with messages that tell us what our lives should look like. What we have now is social media. Now, we can just click an application on our phones and the same messages are "trending." From every angle, we are told that our socioeconomic statuses reflect who we are. Every message carries with it stress, pressure, expectations, violence, and worry. We allow the media to set the standard of living for us. Media has an underlining design to program our lives. I used to wonder why older people referred to television shows as programs. Now I know. Every message that is fed to our minds is created to program us to come back for more garbage. Then, we try to measure up to what the media portrays and compare our lives to our accomplished friends, as well as those on televisions and timelines. And if we don't measure up, we feel less than, worthless and even suicidal, not even understanding that our lives are on a path separate from anyone else's.

FEAR

Fear is a human emotion. Like rejection, it is instilled in us at an early age. Fear is also taught, and that's why I believe it's not as powerful as we make it. Fear can stop us from pursuing a dream, pursuing love and taking calculated risks. On the flip side, it can be used to push us into our destinies. When we don't call fear on its bluff, it can incapacitate our lives. I had a longtime debilitating relationship with fear. Fear caused me to self-sabotage. It kept me from pursuing business startup and other life-changing exploits like writing this book. I was fearful of success and failure. While I am writing this book, I have feel the pressure of fear trying to stop me from writing. What pushes me through the fear is thinking about the people that will be blessed and the lives that will be changed because I decided to tell my story of transformation. I was so entangled with fear that it became the driving force behind my prayer life. That might not be a bad thing. Prayer is good, but we still don't want to live life in fear. "Fear is not real until its power outweighs your courage to move forward"- Joyce Meyer. We have to take our cue from Joyce Meyer and make it happen, even while feeling fear.

The thief will use these devices and more against us. However, as children of God, we have power over these devices. Half the battle is knowing what they are. And Satan can only go as far as we allow him. He can only tempt us. If you are dealing with these devices, don't worry, let me assure you of a few things:

1. You are not the only one experiencing this. You are reading this book because I get it! Remember, I wrote this book as someone who has experienced your same issues. Now that I know how to fight back, I use my personal story of transformation to empower my sisters. I AM YOU!!
2. You are not less than because of it. You must understand that the reason you are a target is because the enemy knows how bright your future is. He knows the treasure you have and he wants it. If you were not going anywhere, you would not be such a threat to the enemy.
3. The enemy has already been defeated. Good thing for you is that you can use the same strategies that Jesus used to defeat him and integrate it with this practical framework.

4. The power you need to step over every device is already within you.

Before your birth, you were equipped for war and for life. Ultimately, the enemy's plan was to use his devices against God's people so that they can choke and become stuck in a place of obscurity. But we are going to cause him to eat his plans.

The Internal Enemy

We help Satan load his weapons when we lack self-awareness, consistency and intention. We also help him load his weapons when we fight each other or water the negative thoughts that he plants in our minds about who we are. The thoughts begin to replay in our hearts until we believe them. But we can also throw those thoughts far out of our minds. Knowledge of your identity means a lot to the enemy. This is why he wants us picked off one by one. Our job is to become adamant about discovering who God is so He can help us to manifest our true identities. In our ignorance, we believe God's plan for our lives means that Satan does not have any plans for us as well. This ignorance causes bondage and leaves us open for attack. I will submit to you that Satan's efforts become more vehement when God has given us a massive responsibility. This is why we should not covet what another person has because we don't know the hell they've experience to get to where they are. In most cases, we are not able to bear the problems another person faces. We were not built for their problems. Neither are we built for their success. In this way, our biggest fight is with ourselves and never with another person.

Yes, you may have been choked by Satan's devices in the past, but now, you will be on the lookout for devices that he may be using against you in particular. They vary from person to person. But, neither tactic can stand a chance against a person who is convinced of their power position. Your knowledge heightens your awareness and his job will not be easy now. Think of it this way: while you are more engrossed in God's purpose for your life, you will learn to use His timeless principles for protection from the powerless devices of the enemy.

CHAPTER 6

Addicted

"Before I formed you in the womb, I knew and approved of you as my chosen instrument and before you were born I separated and set you apart, consecrating you; and I appointed you as a prophet to the nations."
Jeremiah 1:5 [AMP]

It was the end of the eighth-grade school year. You know what that means. I was about to go to high school. No more middle school. It's time to stomp with the big dogs. New clothes, new school, new boys, parties, skating, friends with cars, McDonald's for lunch, freedom and yes, high school sports' tryouts for the upcoming season. And those interested in the school plays or performing in the musical ensemble, there's this in common with the athletes. I was interested in auditioning for the Varsity Drill Team. The drill team is the group of girls who dance in the stands and on the field during the halftime shows while the band played. I thought that I would have a chance because I was already on the Junior Varsity Drill team. We were pretty good. The idea was to get into the high school with the best drill team. At least, that was my reason for wanting to go to Redan High School. I actually didn't have a choice. Redan was the school in my zone. I didn't care about transitioning with my friends. Redan's drill team and band had a great reputation. For some schools, it was basketball and football; for others, it was swimming and baseball.

So, there I was at the Varsity Drill Team tryouts. I knew that my dancing was not the best, but I really wanted to dance. Hopefully, my skill and my moves could withstand the critique of the judges. Being cut from the tryouts is like death. At any level, being cut from a group of selected individuals hurts in more ways than one. This is especially true when the lights are brighter and more people are watching.

While some students were naturally talented enough to be on an athletic team, I know now that the motivation behind trying out for a team was not always skill and ability. That definitely was not the case for me. Athletics was also a way to gain acceptance into certain small groups that existed within the school community. Athletes were the school leaders. In their own right, they had power because teachers and students respected them. The athletic community in the schools closely paralleled the professional athletic world in that the athletes have access to certain things that others don't seem to have access to, such as opportunities and special treatment. They were the school celebrities. So, some students capitalized on the idea of being able to have more friends and more influence from being a student athlete. But what happens when that boy or that girl auditions for a play or shows up to day three of tryouts, only to find out that they have been cut? More often than not, the student feels the normal sting of rejection, especially since they have worked so hard to get to this point. Some of them really have a passion for performing or athletics, but lacked skill or confidence. Either way, it hurts. Rejection is rejection, no matter the reason. And believe me when I tell you, everybody knows who does not make a team because news spreads pretty quickly in high school. I did not make the team during my first or second year, but my effort and commitment helped me land the alternate position; I became the banner girl. I hated being the banner girl. The banner girl held the banner with the school's name in front of the band and looked cute whenever the band had an appearance. To me being the banner girl was equivalent to being "the other woman," which I have been. I did not get the same amount of attention as the "main girls". Neither did I get the respect of the girls who actually made the team. I wanted to dance, not just hold the banner up in front of the band. Plus, I was not auditioning to be a banner girl. To this day, my friends still remind me of being the banner girl. Of, course now I can laugh about it.

Oftentimes, the tryouts are held extensively for days and weeks. Over this period of time, several cuts are made to narrow the list down to the students who exemplify the best skill and have a competitive advantage over the others. Students spent time before and after school perfecting their game, voices, moves, crafts and gathering with other students who were also trying out. They worked with their teachers or coaches to coordinate their schedules. Many of them had close friends cheering them on and holding them accountable. They displayed a level of commitment, energy and dedication to be observed by the judges. They made sacrifices with their schedules to ascertain a certain level of physical and mental preparation for the BIG day. This was kind of a big deal.

High school altogether is a big deal. It was a very defining moment in my life. No matter who you are, these moments come. These are moments when your identity is being shaped and being evaluated. This is when teens start to look for who they are and who they could be. Nevertheless, it's only natural for them to look to friends for the answers. Our friends have a big influence on us. Especially at this stage, self-worth is developed through associations. For this reason, they should be chosen carefully. We go out of the way to gain the acceptance of our friends. Another reason why some students tried out for certain teams was to look for friends or to impress the ones they had. One of the easiest ways to be deeply affected by rejection in high school is to be cut from one of these popular activities. No one wants to look bad in front of his or her friends; this is a sure-fire way to go from impression to depression. A single NO has the power to psychologically destroy a teenager's reputation and his or her ability to have any type of influence at school.

So, here is the whole truth. I wanted to dance. However, more than wanting to dance, I was yearning for attention. I wanted to be affirmed socially because my peers helped me gauge my worth. I thought attention would fill the deep holes that molestation and abandonment left in my heart. It left holes and it stole my value. It left me looking for something to plug those holes. My self-worth was at zero. My associations provided my value and at the time, I did not have many.

The high school experience is infamous for ranking individuals based upon associations, cliques, extracurricular involvement, fashion and smarts. In fact, much of life is based upon performance and rank. We have to live with it, but we must adopt a healthy perspective of it. There are people who are always doing better, looking better, and have better. It's not our job to compete or become jealous of them. We have to let it inspire us to work more aggressively towards purpose. Self-worth was given during creation and is developed through self-discovery. So, looking for it any other way is as futile as chasing a pot of gold at the end of the rainbow. Most importantly, it will never satisfy the void that rejection and hurt leaves in our hearts. It will hinder our personal development.

I wanted people to love me, but deep down inside, I felt like they didn't. I didn't even love myself. Rejection seemed to hurt much more because people who were supposed to protect me inflicted it. These wounds could only be healed by the unconditional acceptance and love of Christ. At the time, I didn't know that. I tried to compensate for the rejection with my conduct, thinking I could fill the void that rejection left. I was tired of being rejected, so I thought that changing what I did would provide immunity from rejection. Due to rejection, I spent most of my life seeking a meaningful identity outside of a true relationship with God.

It Just Got Real

On reveal day, the list went up in the hallway at my high school; it was on display for everyone to see who'd made the teams. Guess whose name was not on it? Mine! Imagine the horror of thinking that something is wrong with you due to a recent rejection. I felt it. Imagine walking into a packed high school lunchroom and all eyes are on you, but not for a good reason. For the next week or so, the whispers did not stop, whether they came from my own head or out of another person's mouth. Immediately, the voices and the lies began to fill my head. The lies usually go something like this, "You will never be anything. You didn't make it because you're not good enough. Now, who will like you? You might as well just take your life." REJECTION. It does not just stop there. It's one thing for the thoughts to come, but we make it worse when we agree with them. We agree with the lies that the enemy suggests by saying, "I'm not good enough," or "Now, nobody will accept me," and "What am I missing?" We open the door for the enemy to walk into. These very thoughts filled my head. The worst part is that I believed them. I made myself easy to be deceived and manipulated. This is when the enemy launches his attack. During moments of vulnerability, our guards are down and an individual is more susceptible to unfavorable treatment. Not to mention that rejection is so foolishly underhanded that it made me feel like something was wrong with me. Had I known some breathing techniques then, I would not have given up my power so freely.

My experiences caused me to believe that I was not worthy of anything better than what I was getting. "A belief is not just an idea that you possess; it is an idea that possesses you." ~John Maxwell. If you can recall, in Chapter 2, we established that identity is the set of BELIEFS, attributes and qualities that give a person their uniqueness. So then, beliefs are a critical component of what shapes a person's identity. If the belief system has been tainted, that person's identity will be in a state of crisis.

In order to breathe better, practice breath awareness. In order to be better, practice self-awareness. In other words, the time is now to come to terms and accept what God says about you. Many can articulate who they are, but their own inner critic or something seemingly stronger than them makes them operate from a place of mistaken identity. Here is a prime example. If your leg was trying to function like your ear, you would have a major dilemma. Your leg has mistaken its identity and therefore, its purpose. And more than that, it might be hard for you to walk or hear. This might also look like someone who makes decisions based on what they think everyone else expects them to be.

Dependency

Talk about mental slavery! I may as well have been locked up behind bars to eliminate the dichotomy between my mind and my body. To be held captive by mental barriers is worlds worse than physical bondage. I can say that because I've been depressed and I know how it feels to be in mental jail. For me, dependency was simply lacking confidence in my inner working. I didn't give myself permission to be abundant and fulfilled.

Another true sign of dependency for me was my habit of giving away my personal authority, thinking that my story and my path were not as important as another person's suggestions, ideas and philosophies. The ability to solve personal problems is hinged on self-discovery. I gave away my personal power to others when I thought that someone else had more power or knowledge than I did about MY life. And my apathy to escape obscurity was tied into the comfort of being average and mediocre.

Jesus' Response to Rejection

Rejection is not a reflection of weakness. Nothing is wrong with you. "NO" is a very common answer and persecution has a specific purpose in your life. Once we come to terms with this truth, we will understand the high levels of warfare. Knowing how to give a NO makes it easier to accept a NO. Furthermore, persecution builds strength and grit. Several times throughout the Bible, Jesus told the disciples that if the people rejected them, it's not personal. He said, "When I send you to a city and you are rejected, kick the dirt off your feet and move to the next city" (Mark 6:11). They rejected Jesus first, but He didn't take it personally. Jesus was resilient, and because we draw our character from Him, we are also resilient.

I, as a result of not being aware of my power, developed the performance mentality, thinking that working to be accepted is equal to gaining respect. While sometimes, I pulled away from people, I was mainly an approval addict. Working to please others and be approved was completely normal for me. I could have worked myself to death with all of the promises I made to people just to gain their approval.

What is Approval?

After rejection my life was characterized by a make-believe need for consent, endorsement, say-so, authorization, or agreement of others. The need for approval does not speak up when necessary. All for the purpose of being liked. This is no way to build relationships. The real way to gain the respect of a person is to be authentic, loyal and by respecting yourself first. People buy into you and you will ultimately attract who you are. So, by no stretch of the imagination does the need for approval gain respect. People who adjust their perspectives to appease me, scare me. This tells me that the appeaser would do anything to get my approval, even if it means lying to me.

I once worked under a boss who had no concept of leadership. By no stretch of the imagination was she a leader. She was very contemptuous and just rude, but she mislabeled her rudeness as realness. She didn't take accountability for any of her wrongs. Of course, I gave into it with my need for approval.

After being on the job for two weeks, I realized that I was dealing with a woman who just held the title of Manager. As a trainee for eighteen months, my job was to learn everything that I could from my "BOSS" in order to develop my skill and knowledge as a professional. She controlled me by manipulation, and I allowed it. Prior to the promotion for this position, I had been with the company for four months. I knew the basics and was beginning to delve into more intricate functions. Being that I am a productivity-oriented person by nature, the transitional period presented a challenge of adjusting. The learning curve seemed insurmountable. Thanks to the BOSS, I had no real training. Let's not forget that the eighteen-month period was for me to obtain training as it related to safety, project management, accounting, category management, negotiations and contract management, amongst other functions. This transitional period was dreadful, but I stuck with it. My boss was so hateful that my co-workers began questioning why I allowed her to treat me the way she did. I was so passive that rather than demanding her respect, I sought after her approval. Somehow, I found myself asking her for permission to do things that I knew I did not need approval for. And I often expressed agreement with things that I did not agree with. Little did I know that this would cause her to disrespect me more. She was a master at taking advantage of my inability to stand up for myself.

One day, as we sat in our daily meeting, I was feeling unproductive because I did not complete an assignment that was given to me the prior week. Prior to the meeting, I'd emailed my boss to solicit her assistance with the project, as it was my first project like this. I had never been tasked with solving a problem of that caliber. Consequently, nothing I did proved to be effective. Nonetheless, I did not give up. I read through the relevant resources, no matter how technical. I endeavored to establish communication among the individuals involved.

As the meeting began, the facility manager circled the conference table as usual for our daily reports on where we were with our individual assignments and departmental projects. In the middle of my response, my boss felt the need to gain control of the dialog between the plant manager and myself as if to say that I could not speak for myself and to suggest that I was not performing my job duties. She never revealed that she'd committed to helping me on the initial assignment, and then reneged. Not to mention again that I was there to be trained. Her assignment while I was there was to expose me to various departmental functions of the facility, to teach me how to anticipate the needs of the facility and guide my development. Instead, she decided to out me during a meeting, claiming that I had not done what she'd told me to do. TALK ABOUT PRESSURE. During this meeting, I became furious, as this was not the first time she'd interrupted me during a meeting. My breathing became rough. I was huffing and puffing, not allowing sufficient oxygen to flow to my brain. I couldn't even take a deep calming breath. Only this time, for some odd reason, I was ready to confront the issue. I kindly told her, "With all due respect, he was talking to me and I am well capable of answering any question that I am asked. In the future, I would appreciate if you did not insult my intelligence by attempting to speak for me." And I continued to answer the question that was directed to me. She later explained that she was under the unscrupulous impression that I was there to take her job and make her look bad. She did not know what else to do, other than to deal with her insecurity in a way that seemingly defended her position. Hence the reason she overcompensated in meetings to impress the plant manager and never fulfilled her responsibility as my trainer; this was at the expense of her reputation.

I believe that her inclination to fight me on such a vehement level was attributed to the male dominated industry that we worked in. Her nature to be guarded and so aggressive was a mechanism she had developed in an attempt to convey to the men that she was the boss, although they may have been the experts of the industry. She wanted them to know that they would not be able to regard her as insignificant, even if she had to humiliate others in the process. I got the impact of it.

On a lighter note, I took a few minutes before the close of that business day to explain to her that I was only there to learn from her, not to take anything away from her. Although she was slightly insecure, she was great at what she did. So, I knew that if I could get her to teach me what she knew, I would be a force to reckon with in the industry. She knew how to perform her job responsibilities like no other. I will give her that, but in the aftermath of what transpired in the meeting, her reaction made me realize that gaining her respect was going to come from standing on my own two feet, rather than seeking her approval. Just to put things into perspective, if I saw her right now, I would wrap my arms around her and offer Christ to her. I admit that I missed the opportunity when we worked together. God wants you to know that He will no longer allow you to bear the burden of guilt for being weak, for living life from a sub-par perspective, or even for not letting your light shine. BREATHE!! You are not a surprise to God. He knows you and that's why He chose you. God believes in you and so should you. Now, He wants you to choose whether it's more beneficial to please people who, by the way, will fail you, people who have the same proclivity to mistakes and failures as you do, or to please the God who has the power to use all of your frailties for the benefit of yourself and others.

"Do not therefore fling away your fearless confidence, for it carries a great and glorious compensation of reward."
Hebrews 10:35

Confidence is the opposite of the need for approval. It's not so much of a skill or as it is the personal validation of your own ability. I can recall having great confidence as a child. I spoke up without being asked. I was not afraid to help people with their perspective, even those who were older and seemingly more knowledgeable. Feelings of competence were always there to help me tackle any situation. Then, I allowed misfortune to steal my confidence. One limiting belief triggered a different outlook. I became frightened by what I thought people would think. I started looking for validation to do what I had been doing. I became silent, knowing that I had answers. Then, I would beat myself up later saying, "Why didn't I just say something?" Lack of confidence really begins to affect our ability to reach our potential or push for anything outside of self.

How To Overcome The Need For Approval?

If you have found yourself seeking approval, no worries. By practicing the following steps, you will develop the mental strength to kick this false need to the curb. Here they are…

Have boundaries that hold yourself and others accountable. I determined that my dedication to a life of service to people is more important than seeking approval. Furthermore, it's hard to really impact lives if I am seeking approval from the same people. It is impossible to hold someone accountable if you are seeking approval. Accountability is characterized by honoring the promises made to yourself first, and requiring others to do the same. On the other hand, the need for approval makes you a target for manipulation. Additionally, when boundaries are enforced, people deliver on their promises and they welcome accountability. It's okay to hold your teachers accountable, hold your mom and dad accountable, hold your boss accountable and hold your spiritual leaders accountable. If a person does not want to be held accountable, the relationship should be re-evaluated. I want people to hold me accountable as well.

Say NO! The word "no" will save your life in more ways than one. I can think of numerous times I've wanted to say no to people, but I said yes, thinking that I would gain their respect. I would say yes to twenty requests, not even considering the others or myself. After that, I would nearly kill myself trying to fulfill every request or, in some cases, I'd renege on my promise and feel like a horrible person. I battled internally because I could not work a miracle. If someone asked me to do something, I would say yes, knowing good and well that I did not want to do it or I had something to do already. A lot of times, we don't know how to tell our friends no because we are so worried about ruining our relationships with them. Guess what? Some of our friends don't mind being told no. It's our personal issues and our own mental barriers that cause us to believe otherwise. Ask yourself this question: Why do I feel the need to be liked? And if they will stop liking you for saying no to them, did they really like you in the first place?

Be true to your views. Being an individual is a true gift that I have not always appreciated. I changed my views to support the majority, conforming, rather than holding my own and fighting for what I believe. You have the freedom to hold your own perspectives, beliefs and philosophies. That's the beautiful aspect of our design. Conversely, those views will be harshly challenged by someone who will have valid points. Not only will views be challenged by people, but they will be challenged by circumstances in general. For instance, it's hard to believe that you are pretty when you have called yourself ugly all of your life. Believing that you will be a millionaire when your bank account is in deficit is a challenge. Believing that I would one day use my bout with severe depression and anxiety to help transform people's lives was a challenge when I was in the pit of depression. Beliefs don't always look like what you see, what you have heard or what you are currently experiencing. However, belief systems determine your viewpoint, expectations, actions and outcomes. God has given us His mind in order that we may have sound reasoning, both creatively and on our own. By this, we can do well in life. Our lives will not exceed our lid for thinking and developing our views.

Immediately confront disrespectful situations. Most people are petrified by the thought of confrontation because confrontation has gotten a bad reputation. I am one who has not seen many amicable confrontations. We just want to give people a piece of our minds and tell them how we feel, but this does not solve the problem or prevent the situation from occurring again. Confrontation is necessary dialog required to move forward with resolve. If done properly, it allows both parties to consider another perspective. The cost of not confronting is expensive, often resulting in broken relationships. We remain paralyzed by situations that could be easily overcome if we were to only confront it in boldness. We allow the fear of confrontation to bully us into silence, preventing growth and development. Confrontation is our job and should be done healthily.

Put your strengths on display. There is a myth that I want to help expose and displace from the minds of all woman, that you should be silent about your strengths. This is a lie! Whoever said this is sadly mistaken. Take it from Marianne Williamson who said,

"Our deepest fear is not that we are inadequate. Our deepest fear is that we are powerful beyond measure. It is our light, not our darkness that most frightens us. We ask ourselves, Who am I to be brilliant, gorgeous, talented, fabulous? Actually, who are you not to be? You are a child of God. Your playing small does not serve the world. There is nothing enlightened about shrinking so that other people won't feel insecure around you. We are all meant to shine, as children do. We were born to make manifest the glory of God that is within us. It's not just in some of us; it's in everyone. And as we let our own light shine, we unconsciously give other people permission to do the same. As we are liberated from our own fear, our presence automatically liberates others."

Most of you have probably heard this thought-provoking and liberating piece, but you have never pulled any revelation from it concerning your own life. Maybe when you read it, there was nothing to relate it to in the present day. All too often, we stumble over the subtle clues that could take our lives from good to great. "But it's just a poem," you may be thinking.
Oh but, it's NOT. It's a poem that speaks to the individual purpose that we were given.

What she emphatically tells us is our greatest concern in life has nothing to do with whether or not we are good enough. The real fear is knowing that we ARE capable of executing our calling in ways that are more powerful than we've ever imagined. You literally have the power to change cities, nations and regions in a way that is pleasing to God, and in a way that would allow you to make an impact and live abundantly. Fear might never go away. Success is still possible with fear being present.

You are an original. You have a story that can be used to transform and inspire. You are a carrier of the "Glory of God" due to the fact that you were made in His image. His glory within you is seeking expression and you should put it on display. You are a light. Lights are not made to be hidden. Your shining light will help others to shine.

Downplaying your strengths is not what God intended for you. You can't change the world with a dim light. You were wired for greatness so anything less than that will cause misalignment because it does not support the significance of your creation. Embrace what makes you unique, even if it makes others uncomfortable. Shrinking back to pacify the insecurities of others counteracts the opportunity to have an impact and ultimately ends up contributing to the plight of our society.

Develop a growth mindset. People who maintain a growth mindset are continuously making strides to get to the next milestone, rather than being stopped by obstacles. I like to call them D.U.M.B. They are DELIBERATE, UNSTOPPABLE, MENTALLY MOTIVATED AND BRILLIANT. They attack every day with deliberation. They do what is necessary to stay motivated over the long haul. Star athletes and millionaires have mastered this mindset. When you enter the growth mindset, your fulfillment will come with your progress rather than with gaining approval from others. Your own potential will be at the forefront of your mind with every step forward. A growth mindset helps to eliminate the chatter of what others think.

Give people what they really want. What if I told you that people are in need of what you have? They want you to give them a gift! The answers and the gifts that are locked up inside of you are what they are after. That's why you are obligated to discover your reason for being alive. Stop taking their disapproval of you personally. In Chapter 12, you will learn my formula to discovering and activating your purpose and you will discover one of the most amazing people living—YOU.

Our responsibility is to please God. People are the beneficiaries of our main commitment to God. It's about bringing attention to God by pioneering a movement and a culture of empowerment and self-discovery amongst each other. Disapproval comes with being human. Therefore, whether you are doing right or wrong, someone is going to disapprove you. Your job is to give people permission to disapprove you, so that when it happens, you can continue to move forward. Or you will always be unhappy and trying to fit a mold. If your happiness is at the hand of another imperfect human being, you don't have control of your life.

One of the ways respect is acquired is from teaching people how to treat you and working to build mutually beneficial relationships. Your life will only attain the value in which you have invested. We can't expect the value of life to exceed what we've put into it. In actuality, most of us believe that one of the characteristics of a friend is agreement with everything they say and do, but that's not friendship. There is such a thing as disagreement. But here is a caveat, you can disagree without being unpleasant and distasteful. We don't have to always agree to maintain a healthy relationship. Doing so, we'd find ourselves babysitting relationships that were based on unrealistic expectations from the beginning. If everyone around you agrees with you, how are you growing? Are you being challenged? Life is so much more interesting when you feel confident enough to use your freedom of expression, opinion to have educated conversations and challenge others to see something from another vantage point.

The most successful people of the world reached the pinnacles of success by surrounding themselves with people who challenged their way of thinking. Clever people surround themselves with people smarter and more accomplished than themselves because they understand that iron sharpens iron. There is a mutual benefit to being in the company of other clever people, where there is a continuous sharing of knowledge. World-class teams are built on this concept. You NEED people who are smarter than you, people who will challenge your thinking process. These people will not always agree with you. You are not growing if you are the smartest person in the room. How boring life would be if there were no challenges to address? This is where the appreciation of diversity and diverse meaningful opinions begin.

Can I share something personal with you? God knows everything about you and He still approves of you, although he may not be happy with all of your choices. He knows the silent fears and the insecurities that you try to hide. He also knows that you will hardly do everything right and He still approves of you. Once you accept God's approval of you, the courage to lead in your area will manifest and you will be able to operate beyond what you have been accustomed to. God wants you to enjoy an enriching relationship with Him. You can't do this when you are seeking the approval of people.

You don't have to be ashamed of any trial, weakness or proclivity that you have or have had. God can use anything, even an addiction. Now, you have to approve of yourself. You have not been disqualified. There is still a gift that God placed in you, but now, clarity, along with your acceptance of the truth, will bring acceleration. You can take all of the years of your addictions and bad habits, add them all together and God approves of who you are and provides grace to live effectively.

CHAPTER 7

When Depression and Anxiety Attacks

"The worse our breathing habits are, the closer we are to our own death. The good news is that we can easily improve the way we breathe and reverse a negative health trend at any age"
~Anders Olsson

Most would agree that breathing takes more attention than they thought. When it comes to breathing, babies and children do it properly and without struggle. In ideal situations, babies are born completely healthy and have no obstruction in their breathing. So, optimal breathing is normal for them. As a child matures into adulthood, responsibilities increase, so does stress and the tendency to become out of balance emotionally and mentally. The psychological imbalance causes chaotic breathing. Many don't consider conscious breathing until normal breathing becomes a struggle. This is because people are unaware that practicing proper breathing techniques daily can make all the difference in the quality of their lives. This type of awareness requires a mental shift. What once took no thought becomes something that has to be managed daily.

Initially, when I started the outline for this book, I was extremely depressed. I found myself facing a quarter-life crisis. According to clinical psychologists, a quarter-life crisis is a period of time where those who are between the ages of 18 and 35 experience insecurity, disappointment and doubt surrounding their lives, relationships, career paths and finances. This definition could not describe my situation more clearly. I defined myself by what I did not have, who I was not and what I was not doing. I created dysfunction for myself by comparing myself and chasing something that I was never meant to have. The sentiments and symptoms that I was having confirmed the research performed by doctors, which also states that the key challenges that millennials face include identity confusion, internal conflict and uncertainty. Coupled with the symptoms above, I was questioning my identity, I was unproductive, unfulfilled and misaligned. I even wondered if there was a place for me in my family and in this world.

I doubted that God loved me or that there was a real purpose for my life. I wanted to be as accomplished as other people I saw who were my age. I never considered that people who I saw as publically successful are prone to suicidal ideations, silent contemplations of dread and doubt they even matter. I tried to measure up to a social definition of well-being. Measuring up is rooted in comparison and competition and is an attempt to do what another person is doing or get what another person is getting because of the seemingly beneficial outcome, usually superficial. One who compares themselves to others is, in essence, rejecting who God made them to be. What I needed to do was level-up. To level-up is to use your internal power (confidence, mental strength, emotional intelligence, competence) to defy the odds that are stacked against you, in a way that will cause continuous personal development. Trying to measure up got me nowhere because it canceled out my individuality.

One factor that contributed to my depression was being in college for so long. I remember thinking, "All of my friends have graduated. I am still in school and graduation day is nowhere in sight. There has to be more to life than this." I was working on one degree for ten years. I felt like I had to catch up with everyone who lapped me. Granted, I sat a few semesters out. I was becoming a grown up with real responsibilities and still working on the same degree, repeating classes and changing my major. The only thing that really made me want to finish was that I did not want to be the person who would start and stop things in my life and never finish. Plus, I was trying to live the American dream; that is, graduate from college, get a job, and buy a house with a white picket fence.

Even the American Dream is limiting, considering that I was made for more than to just work a job and pay a mortgage. When I reflect on the reason I was depressed, on top of the clinical reasons, one of them is because I subscribed to the "American system." I allowed myself to believe that if I did not obtain a certain lifestyle by a certain year, then I must be worthless. What a silly misconception, considering that America does not know half the woman I am and will not contribute to the woman I could become. I let my attempt to fit into the American dream deprive me of the proper breath that I needed to charge forward into fearless pursuit of purpose. I never knew the importance of purpose. No one ever emphasized it. People always asked, "What do you want to be when you grow up?" or "Where do you work?" Those questions increase the pressure to consider economic potential, rather than purpose. Why do we feel the need to conform to the American System? College is not for everyone, especially those who are not clear about what they want to do. I could have saved so much time, energy and tens of thousands of dollars had I majored in my identity before I choose a major of study. That's the thing. We spend so much time studying to become experts in an area of study and neglect ourselves the opportunity to know if the chosen major will optimize our inherent gifts. I limited myself to graduating and finding a job. So, even when I did graduate and find a job, I was miserable because there was so much more inside of me that I suppressed because I was chasing something that I was not sure I wanted.

What Depression and Anxiety are Really Like

Not only was I depressed, I was anxious and stressed. Depression and anxiety are partners in crime and they tag teamed against my life until I was backed into a corner. I lost interest in things that I would normally enjoy. My sleep patterns were disrupted. Anxiety said, "If you sleep, you die," so I went days without even going to sleep at night. Since I wanted to stay alive, I listened to those evil thoughts. Sometimes, from miles away, my mom had to pray over me until I fell asleep. On other days, I had to find the energy to open my eyes and crawl out of bed. I had stuff to do. People think that symptoms of depression are relegated to being in bed all day and closed off from the world. I still had to get up, put on my public persona and go to work. After making it to work, I had to then function and perform a job.

I was worried about my image at the expense of my dying soul. I worked on my image until what really mattered was not even in my view. I did not want anyone to know that I could be facing such a real thing. Some nights, I sat up and cried myself to sleep, and I cried myself to and from work. Living in two of the most beautiful states meant nothing because depression and anxiety consumed the experience.

I was good at looking like I had it together. That was easy. I could look like I was confident and act like it too. I was able to act so well that I even became an actor. LITERALLY! I made people think that my spices were in alphabetical order in my cabinet, but behind closed doors, I was a mess. My self-worth was tied to my career, which had just begun, and my connections, who liked me. My purpose was not even a priority for me; it was on the back burner.

Anxiety is inner turmoil characterized by worry and caused by fear. It will paralyze your thoughts so you won't do what you know to do. Anxiety caused me to settle when I knew that I wanted and deserved more and it caused me to decline an important phone call that I had been expecting. Anxiety caused me to disregard goals that would move my life forward. Anxiety caused me to quit the dream job that I asked God for and then, turn around and hate myself for doing it. Anxiety is waking up in the morning, thinking about how dreadful the day will be. I've also spent time making plans for a trip or to attend an event, only for anxiety to cancel my plans. Anxiety simply does not believe that something can go well.

When depression and anxiety tag team the inner dialog sounded like this:

"Don't fail or mess up today, everybody is watching."

"I am a failure and God will never forgive me if I mess up."

"I'm going to die today."

"The world is better off without me; my family will not even miss me."

"That last break-up was my fault. I may as well give up on relationships because no one loves me."

"I am going to get sick and die if I don't kill myself first."

One erroneous thought supports another erroneous thought. These erroneous thoughts shaped my self-esteem and became my identity. Coupled with the thoughts, I felt drained and I had no strength to function effectively. I did not want to go to work or school. I isolated myself from my friends, those who were genuinely concerned about my well-being. Isolation is the worst place to be while depressed. But sometimes, having people around heightened the depression because I had to fake like I was okay until they left.

I was so anxious and fearful about my future that my inner turmoil began to cause anxiety attacks. One thought attacked the integrity of my breath. I would be sitting at my desk and suddenly began panting and gasping for air. There was one time in particular where I'd made it to my car in time enough to get my mom and aunt on the phone, and they had to perform an intervention. They have no training in mental health or first aid, but they did what they knew to do spiritually. They tag-teamed on what had been tag teaming against me. They prayed and began to speak to the spirit of anxiety as if it were a person. It spoke to me like a person, so why not? Suddenly, I began to catch my breath. Prayer is definitely a part of treatment. However, professional help was necessary for my transformation. I have experienced all types of pain in my life. Out of all the pain that I have ever felt, including physical pain, I truthfully think depression and anxiety are the worst pains I have experienced. I would not wish this pain on my worst enemy.

Self-inflicted Anxiety

In a world where stress and overwhelm are customary, we choose toxic lifestyles and wonder why anxiety is on our trail. If I can be honest, I've added to stressful stimuli, creating more severe levels of disorder and dysfunction in my life. I made extremely toxic decisions, including staying involved in unhealthy relationships. These decisions were contrary to the life of peace and courage that I was wired for. I did not display self-control with my mouth, actions, schedule, money, eating, or friends, so my life was out of control. I contributed to my own dysfunction when I let my life succumb to a flow, rather than deliberately deciding what I should do with my time, money, and thoughts. My poor decisions brought about results that placed my mind into disorder. My experience with depression was partly the result of making poor decisions. When I knew to do right, I chose to do wrong.

Toxic schedules and electronics create the perfect environment for anxiety to live. Morning routines characterized by waking up in time enough to check emails, direct messages (DM's) and text messages before running out of the door create stress. Each type of communication is laced with expectations. We don't have systems that would help us to function optimally. We go to stressful jobs, don't take lunch breaks (thinking breaks decrease productivity), and then, we fall asleep to the sound of toxic news, on top of the work we bring home.

The Journey

Finally, the day came that I graduated from college. After graduation, I immediately moved to Texas, where I had always wanted to live. On paper, everything was pretty good. I was working a great job and I had my own place once again. I could afford my rent and I could afford to save as well. But, I was still depressed. I was not fulfilled or happy. This was all because I was doing what I thought people would admire. It was more important for me that people thought I was doing well than to really be doing well. No one really knew I was depressed because, at my core, I'm a really upbeat, loving and outgoing person. But I was not myself.

All I could think about was how I was never going to go back to Atlanta. I felt like being away from Atlanta was removing me from my negative emotions. I was wrong. Everything followed me, even the negative emotions that I never acknowledged. I couldn't seem to get away from myself, no matter where I went. It's almost like the people who want to live in gated communities who think that they will lock all of the criminals and villains out. Perhaps the villain is on the inside of the gate. Then, where do you go? I was alone. I did not know anyone. I moved to escape my past. God had another thing coming my way. He moved me away to discover myself. First, I got a chance to face myself. Self-examination is extremely uncomfortable. I needed discomfort to push me forward. I didn't want to face it then, but it was the best thing I could ever do. Things got worse before they got better. At first, my time alone was almost unbearable, because I did not know how to love myself properly. I knew that I did not want to stay this way. And still, there was an ever-so-present nagging love from God that would not let me give up.

Even though I sometimes felt completely detached, I had my faith to depend on. My mom instilled faith in me growing up. Instilled faith in me is a cute way to say it, after all, we really had no choice. If my mom was at church, we were at church. If she prayed at home, we prayed. She put her faith on display, so I knew where to turn for help. I knew that it was time for me to reassess my spiritual life, career path, and what was important to me. I needed help, so I sought psychological help and was soon after diagnosed with severe depression. I can remember thinking "Oh my goodness, I am depressed!" The diagnosis sparked a longing in me that made me want to live. I remember thinking, "If I am going to have any type of real success in my life, I need to make some changes." So, I did. I was tired of crying myself to sleep or staying up all night to keep from dying. I did everything that my psychologist told me to do. I took online courses and forgiveness courses, I created a daily routine, created a meditation schedule, started journaling and prayed more. I read books on overcoming depression and increasing self-esteem, but I also dealt with the root: I worked on identity discovery. I didn't want to just get a remedy for the depression and leave all of the other problems. I wanted a complete transformation. I really needed to pull on my upbringing in faith. I went to the Word of God to find the truth about myself. I wanted God to answer some questions for me, so I asked Him, "God, who am I? Why did you create me? Where am I going from here?"

I often wondered if my life was going to succumb to my thoughts. Am I the broken promises that I made to people? Am I the lies that I told or the broken relationships that I was once a part of? Am I the squandered opportunities? Am I my job and my connections? Am I this major depression disorder that I am dealing with? Who am I? This couldn't be it. I needed some help figuring this one out.

I had never expected an answer back the way I did in that moment. It was as if God was waiting on me to ask the question. He began to point me to scriptures in the Bible that were stamps of my identity. After a while, I think I found all of them. Learning one created a hunger for more. I ran closer to God and He came closer to me.

Here are 24 verses to serve as a reminder of who you are in Christ.

1. I am fearfully and wonderfully made in the image of God. Psalms 139:15
2. I am free from condemnation. Romans 8:1
3. I am God's workmanship, created in Christ Jesus to do good works. Ephesians 2:10
4. I am hidden in the secret place of the Most High. Psalms 91:1
5. I am a new creature in Christ. 2 Corinthians 5:17
6. I am the light of the world. Matthew 5:14
7. I am the salt of the earth. Matthew 5:13
8. I am transformed by the renewing of my mind. Romans 12:2
9. I am the righteousness of God. 2 Corinthians 5:21

10. I am the daughter of a King and a joint heir with Christ. Romans 8:17, 2 Corinthians 6:18
11. I am accepted in the beloved. Ephesians 1:6
12. I am complete in Christ. Colossians 2:10
13. I am redeemed, forgiven and free from the power of sin. Galatians 3:13, Ephesians 1:7, Romans 6:14
14. I am a member of a chosen generation and a royal priesthood for God. 1 Peter 2:9
15. I am strong in the Lord in the power of His might. Ephesians 6:10
16. I am an overcomer. Revelation 12:11
17. I am blessed with all spiritual blessings in heavenly places. Ephesians 1:3
18. I am more than a conqueror and victorious through my Lord Jesus Christ. Romans 8:37, 1 Corinthians 15:57
19. I am secure, far from oppression and fear, and terror will not come near me. Isaiah 54:14
20. I am the head and not the tail; above not beneath. Deuteronomy 28:13
21. I have the mind of Christ. 1 Corinthians 2:16
22. I am prospering in every area of my life 3 John 2:1
23. I am sealed by the Holy Spirit with promise. Ephesians 1:13
24. I am healed by His stripes. Isaiah 53:5

This list doesn't just reveal my identity, it reveals your identity! Although these scriptures are universally known, they must become personal to you. More than learning my identity, I had to believe it. That's where the struggle came. Reciting the scriptures was a piece of cake, but believing the scriptures were true about me took some time. Repetition was the key to seeing results. To breathe better, I had to consistently practice better breathing habits. Before I knew this, I was gasping chaotically.

Overall, God created us for one reason, and that's to be a prototype of Him in the Earth. You also have an assignment as a woman, and most importantly, as an individual. There is a problem that your family and your generation will face that makes your existence during this time very necessary. When I thought about asking God why I had to go through what I went through, God asked me, "How would you be able to help others overcome depression if you never overcame it yourself?" This is what I heard so clearly when I asked God. He also told me this.

"I created you to be a representation of me in the Earth. You will be the closest resemblance of me that some people will meet. You will be a rescuer and a strategist who provides solutions to women during their most difficult times. Your answers will provide protection and freedom. You will agitate and confront what has always been. You will be a voice for the voiceless. You will help people optimize the power of their minds. You are counsel!"

He did not say this all at once, but He showed me visions of myself accomplishing each assignment. This is not limited to me. I represent you and I believe that you and I share in that we have an assignment as representatives for our Father.

I asked myself, "Where am I going from here?" This is a question about the future. Only I could determine the answer. At the time, I wanted to see myself on the other side of depression and on the other side of man's opinions. THAT'S IT. Deep inside, I knew there was more, but it was buried by all of the limiting beliefs I had and everything else that I'd memorialized. You get to choose where you go. God sets before you a good life and a mediocre life. He gives you freewill to choose which life you want to live. Knowing who you are and knowing why you were created will help you to know where you are heading.

Why did God create me? Where am I going? Who AM I? My life was controlled by the inability to answer these questions. No one else could answer them for me, not even the psychologist that I'd paid. Each question is a self-discovery question that reveals identity. I used all of the treatments that the psychologist provided, but nothing cured my crisis like me being able to answer these questions. God and His Word led me to the answers and provoked me to pay close attention to the needs of my soul. I had to find myself in the words that I read on the pages about my identity. It became my safety and a treasure chest of answers for my life. Do I feel like I'm "above and not beneath" every day? Do I always feel "strong in the Lord"? The answer is a resounding NO. Some days, I feel weak, but I am able to be led by truth, rather than feelings. When I embrace my weaknesses, God can be strong for me.

"And you will know the Truth and the Truth will set you free"
John 8:32

The enemy uses various weapons to attack our identities. According to Romans 7:23, we learn that there is a different force at work, making you a prisoner to the law of sin. We talked about this earlier when I gave you the devices that he often uses against us. For me, these attacks often came in the form of a circumstance that led me to depression, discouragement, or even disillusionment. In these situations, I'd attempted to quit —to walk off the field and surrender. Certainly, the enemy is coming after you too, but in a different way. You have the power to overcome every temptation and make choices that are in alignment with your true identity. Victory has already been slated for you. Once you win, don't just think about how bad the experience was. TAKE THE REWARDS! Every victory permits the possession of wisdom, courage, hope, and muscle for the next fight. The spoils can be used for personal restoration and then, to light the way for those who are on a journey to freedom.

Depression is not a hopeless situation. But, many clinicians withhold such information to preserve the earning power of the billion-dollar stress industry. Masking depression with medication and receiving therapy that would cause a cognitive shift are different. Therapy confronts the root of depression through strategic questioning, repetition and commitment. A therapist seeks to understand a person in their context to discover where the breakdown happened. They ask questions like: how much you love what you do? When was the last time you experienced happiness? What situations took place before your happiness vanished? What should I know about your childhood experiences? Who are you outside of your job and title? What are your daily habits? Do you live by your personal convictions? What do you love? What are your challenges? Do you have clarity on who you are and your purpose? What have you tried? Do you have any goals set? What does your ideal day look like?

I am not mocking the healthcare industry. I believe in doctors and healthcare professionals. However, we can't be dismissive of facts that surround why people may be experiencing depression. The causes of depression are not limited to genetics and chemical imbalances. Life experiences have the ability to cause depression. However, toxic thought patterns that are suggestive of a depressive state are not an automatic diagnosis of a disorder. Sometimes, we are not even depressed, we may be exasperated from toiling and working so hard to make others happy. You could very well be experiencing sadness. There is a very suggestive difference. Either way, the emotions suggest that care should be taken to re-align with the proper way of thinking.

Your life does not have to be branded by a traumatic experience. If we begin to ask the questions that uncover the root cause, we'll discover that depression can be traced back to a traumatic life experience, which was ignored and has re-emerged as feelings of hopelessness, toxic thought patterns and undesirable behaviors. More than the traumatic experience, the irrational views that are developed cause the most damage to the individual. Overtime, the distorted views grow into mental illness if not acknowledged. I am boldly suggesting that mental illness can be healed as God has created every human being with mind power. This type of healing will require consistency, patience and commitment. The individual will also have to understand a very rudimentary principle by appreciating progress and growth. Otherwise, the primitive desire to want an easy and sudden fix will pervade the motivation. Romans 12:2 contends that all transformational power comes from your mind. This text further supports my belief that you don't have to live with depression if you don't want to.

As much as we hate to admit it, sometimes the state of our mental health is the direct result of daily choices. Whenever we behave in ways that are juxtaposed to our intended design, we open our minds to chaos. For example, lack of self-acceptance, gossip, resentment, shrinking back, fear and people-pleasing contribute to an unhealthy mindset.

We Can All Win

As women, we learn our responsibility to nurture. Overtime, nurturing starts to look like making excuses for the toxic decisions of others or playing small, and not releasing our gifts to the world. Sometimes, we sabotage our wins when others don't seem as opportune. We genuinely want to see everyone winning. That's a good personal characteristic, but not when the consequence is guilt for being successful. The truth is we all can win. And this has to be our perspective and mindset. We must be able to share our accomplishments in a way that is humble to show sensitivity to each other. Sharing wins and strategy provides a platform. People will want to know your step-by-step process. This is the group of people who you will influence and nurture. You will inspire them to inspire others. They have your ear and they value your expertise. For a business owner, this is your target market. You might get some outside of this group who will support you, but this is the main group who will read your blogs, listen to your podcasts, come to your conferences and demand your intellectual property, as well as other resources. They should be your focus, and this is ultimately your assignment. You no longer need validation. Purpose validates you!

One of the effects of depression that I often experienced was shortness of breath. The medical term is Dyspnea. In short, it means dysfunctional breathing. Some days, I would wake up and it felt like an elephant had been standing on my chest. Other times, I had panic and anxiety attacks throughout the day while I was at work. Similar to the choking episodes, I would be overtaken with intense fear, triggered by a thought that caused my breathing to become heavy and chaotic.

One horrible tendency that stopped me from getting the help I needed for so long was that I was prideful. Only pride will stop someone from getting the help needed when their life is threatened. There is this stigma that causes us to be ashamed if we need help. All I had to say was, "I CAN'T BREATHE." I wanted them to just know. You are likely more courageous than I am. I often ponder the question: How many of us are, in so many words, telling our doctors, friends or family members that we can't breathe, but to no avail? We are telling doctors and other medical practitioners our symptoms, and rather than tracing the symptoms to the root to find a real cure, they are just medicating the symptoms with false hope. The problems are worsening. In my mind, the only way to defeat it was to become intentional and take an active role in my recovery. Even if I did tell others, my recovery was up to me. Once I began to gain control over my mind and face my pain, my truth changed and healing started. Once my mind changed, my behaviors changed. It did not happen overnight. I had to commit to a rigorous but beneficial process. My process has now become my lifestyle.

You have a great assignment to complete and the enemy will try to impede it. He will try to tempt you into bad choices so that your thinking can be afflicted, but you have the power to rise above his temptation and his attacks. He has no more power than what you give him.

A thought pattern that is characterized by disorder and chaos, can be reversed back to order with very practical and intentional routines. Here are some…

1. Develop a morning routine. Wake up and set an intention for the day. Before you look at your emails, text messages and schedule, give thanks to God for another day. Pray and

ask Him to lead and guide your day, and to allow you to function at your best in every situation.

2. Attack every day with intention. Prepare food, clothes and schedules for the week so that your days will not be carried out in real time.
3. 3. Develop a nighttime routine. Wind down before you actually go to sleep. Eat dinner, go for a walk or read a book. Disconnect from all electronic devices about thirty minutes to an hour before you go to bed. Life will kick in, and may not always be feasible, but do your best to eliminate as much stressful stimuli as possible. Don't go to sleep to bad news. Don't let the television or any other negative program play in the background. Negativity will contribute to your thought patterns. Your ears are the gates to your mind. So, whatever you allow in will express itself in your thoughts.
4. Implement study and scriptural meditation as a part of your morning and nighttime routine. Meditation does not interfere with your Christian faith. Meditation is a biblical principle of prosperity and health. It helps me to train myself to think positively and improves my attention. Grasping control of your thoughts is a skill that comes with practice and meditation provides the practice. It leads you into the peaceful presence of God. Start with seven to ten minutes in the morning and the same before bed.
5. Remove yourself from toxic relationships. In a toxic relationship, you will find yourself putting in all of the work to maintain the relationship. These are relationships where you are being manipulated and your boundaries are not being respected. Also, if you find that being around certain people causes you to feel toxic at the end of the day, avoid them at all costs. If you must work with them, you control the interactions you have with them.
6. Pray. Prayer is the sure-fire way to change any aspect of your life that you are working to change.
7. When you feel depression in its onset, try to trace it back to the thought that caused it. If you can identify the trigger,

you can deal with it from the root. Do not allow it to bully you into silence. Take action

8. Make good decisions. FORGIVE, be polite, obey what God tells you to do, have pure intentions. “Depression is fed by poor decision-making” ~Dr. Caroline Leaf
9. Seek professional counsel. Don’t try to deal with this alone if you feel defeated. Understand that your recovery is up to you. It might seem easier to just let things stay the way they are, but the damage is actually worsening. Trusted professionals are available.
10. Stop comparing yourself to others. Become so interested in your own work that you get satisfaction from a job well done. Then, you will not feel the need to compare yourself to anyone (Galatians 6:4 NLT). If you are always comparing what you are doing and who you are to another person, defeat and depression will be the result.

If you are productivity-oriented like me, you will look for immediate results. Don’t become defeated when results are not immediate. Slow and steady wins the race. It took a while to wire dysfunction into your mind, so it might take time to reverse.

I love the fact that I can write to you as you. Had I not been depressed, I don’t think I would have gone after God and purpose so aggressively. I admit that I needed something to scare me into my purpose. That does not have to be the case for you. I actually believe that God is breaking down walls of fear, limiting beliefs and intimidation, and He is raising up a generation of women who will produce a culture of identity awareness. These women will start at an early age, having no doubt or apprehension about their REAL identities. I don’t know what in particular has taken your breath, but what I do know is that it is God's will for you to be revived.

CHAPTER 8

Lies

Stop believing the lies about who you are so you can create the most powerful version of yourself.

"When we repeat an action often enough, it soon becomes a habit. Once we have established incorrect breathing patterns, we risk them becoming permanent, which can cause added stress, lack of oxygen and energy shortage."
~Anders Olsson

Have you ever believed something for so long that it seemed true, then when you were made aware of the truth you, were able to take a breath of fresh air? The truth is, many people don't know who they are because they have believed lies for so long that the lies have become their truth. Whether good or bad, we are all the sum total of our beliefs. The foundation of our beliefs start in the home or not too far from it and at a young age. The early stages of life are critical to our development. In the home, our view of the world is shaped. We believed parents and other trusted individuals. We leaned into their care, hoping that our childhood grooms us to become prospering and well-balanced adults. We hope that the reason behind being told NO has a more sensible aim than, "because I said so." As a child none of this makes sense, but as a mature adult, appreciation is retrospectively demonstrated.

Life starts off being reared by parents, but the way nature has it, the responsibility is shifted to the developing person. It's safe to say that well-being is shaped by childhood experiences, although childhood is not the only factor that contributes to overall well-being. Similarly, proper breathing habits are shaped during childhood. So, the reason that some adults have poor breathing habits are a direct result of the negative ideas that were instilled into their minds as children. A healthy psychological view of self has not been developed in some cases, because of a forcible indoctrination of wrong beliefs. Some are still living life, married to fairy tales, nursery rhymes or the lies learned from childhood … lies that affect breathing and blur our vision. We don't have a healthy perception of who we are so our happiness and overall well-being are both threatened. Therefore, breathing is threatened.

It has been argued that nursery rhymes set to music aid in a child's development. Research also supports the assertion that music and rhyme increase a child's spatial reasoning, which aid mathematics and communication skills. As I child, I enjoyed learning in a fun environment. Most children do. I love nursery rhymes due to the goal behind it, but if the lines of the nursery rhyme are meant to be sweet and fuzzy without validity, they can and have had unpleasant ramifications. While nursery rhymes definitely have the tendency to develop a child's literacy skills, the fun and games become a nightmare when kids grow up believing the words to the rhymes … words that have no soundness or logical context for emotional development. For this reason, nursery rhymes should only be utilized to do just as the name denotes… RHYME.

One nursery rhyme says that we are made of sugar and spice and everything nice, and boys are made of snips and snails and puppy dog tails. This is a lie. I don't like being lied to. It's a cute way of engaging a child to help them understand a concept, but the content has no relevance to the true identity that God created and gave because it's contrary to His image. Like so many other things we learned as children, it's just not true. Hence, one of the reasons many women and men alike are struggling to be fulfilled, and are constantly believing the lie that something is permanently wrong with them. I think that nursery rhymes are brilliant; sometimes, we need parables and other literary devices to aid in our learning, but to dumb down who we really are to teach a false concept will never render favorable results. The creativity and brilliance of God are to be put on display and not diluted and weakened. He did His absolute best work when He created you.

Psalm 139 says that you were intricately and skillfully formed as if embroidered with many colors in the depths of the earth. God was very meticulous about your creation. He even says that the hairs on your head are numbered. Nothing about sugar, spice or everything nice encourages me like knowing that I am fearfully and wonderfully made in the image of Christ. Who, other than God, knows those intimate details of your creation? You were literally made from dirt and then formed into a beautiful masterpiece.

This speaks to God's masterful creative abilities. Providing partial truths to promote an understanding is not wise; it only creates confusion. So, if we are going to create rhymes or easy ways to help us understand something, we should use parables like Jesus did and teach from a true premise. This helps us to aid people's processes and journeys to live happy and fulfilled lives. We are not made of snips and snails and puppy dog tails, neither are we made of sugar and spice and everything nice. God made all of those things, but He did not use either of them to create you or me. He used dirt that was moistened from morning dew. This may not be your story in particular because some people have never heard this rhyme, but keep reading and maybe you can identify with one of the lies that have played into our mental conditioning. This is just a metaphor. We first have to recognize that they are lies about who we are.

You may have been told, "You're just like your father" or "You're just like your mother." Your parents may be genuinely great people that inspire your major life-decisions, as they should be. However, you are still not them. Genetically, you carry their traits, but you will take a completely different path. No one else out of the seven billion people on Earth has your perspectives, skillsets or gifts in the same way that you do, not even your parents. While there are role models that we can learn from, our lives will all take different trajectories. We are individuals and are created to operate from that position.

"You are just like your father," sounds fairly harmless to most people, but ends up being an emotional blow to the receiver. The impact behind this statement has the power to be psychologically harmful. My dad did not have a superlative reputation. So being told, "You're just like your father" was not what I wanted to hear. I am not judging him. I loved my dad with all of my heart. He was a creative. I get my sense of humor from him, but he was not the person who I wanted to model my life after, if I can be honest. So, I did not want to be told that I would be just like him. Growing up, I remember people saying this, and surely, they meant well. Unfortunately, the only reference points that I had were my trips to visit him in jail. As a child, my thought was that he must have done something bad, which made him a bad person. My dad was in jail for all of my childhood and most of my life. So, every time I heard those words, "You're just like your daddy," I felt the impact of those words—words that subconsciously formed what I believed about myself and even some of the behaviors that I adopted.

My family actually did a good job at not really discussing my dad's situation with me. I don't believe I would have been able to handle the truth at such a young age, especially without counseling to follow up. I just knew he was in jail. Most children know what jail is and why people go there, so I could make certain deductions and connections about the type of person that I thought my dad was. This was one of the things that I was able to trace my rejection, anger and shame back to when I began to self-examine myself and soul search. For a while, I thought I would end up like my dad, and I made myself believe that no one cared how I turned out.

I learned why my dad was in jail when I became a young adult, when I was able to search him in an online database. I remember visiting my dad in the various jail facilities as a child. I remember writing letters and getting cards for my birthdays and special holidays. My mom did a great job keeping me in his life. That's the only reason I really knew who my dad was. I also remember making trips to the crack house as an adult to visit him when he was out of jail. He got out and then went back repeatedly and this cycle never ended.

You might have been told, "You should be ashamed of yourself," and that's exactly what you have become. Parents and people in general are known for saying this phrase. It is one of the most hurtful things that can be said to a person, especially to a child. Shame is a negative emotion that causes feelings of worthlessness. People who say this phrase usually don't have malicious intentions when they say it, but the person on the receiving end gets the brunt. Sometimes, making the statement does not seem so harmful because it serves the purpose of creating awareness of disrespect. That's important. We need to be checked sometimes. If, I can be honest, I need to be. However, there are simply better ways of pointing out intolerable behavior. This ways is so emotionally hurtful, because people grow up and live addicted to shame all because someone told them they should be that way. We want people to learn from their mistakes, but we should always encourage people to love themselves while they are in the process of correction.

Shame is so powerful because it broods over toxic decisions while restricting the person you could be. It causes the inability for us to gain clear insight of our good qualities after a poor decision. For so long, I dimmed any impact that I could make focusing on my shortcomings.

You may have been told, "You are a failure" or "You'll never be able to do that." No one ever said that you would not fail. However, even if you fail, you are scheduled for a comeback. God can turn cycles of failure in to a lifetime of success.

Imagine having a great idea and not being able to execute it because you have been told that you will not succeed. While I believe that we should make calculated decisions, what I know for sure is that another person's failure's or even your past failures will not eliminate future success. If that were the case, many of the people who you admire would not be successful. They are known for accomplishing what some have tried to no avail.

Were you told, **"You are a mistake"**? The result of this statement is detrimental and definitely inflicts feelings of rejection. If you have not been told this, just imagine that you know someone who has been. One can only expect their soul to be hanging on by a thread. Children told that they are a mistake will likely grow up more susceptible to manipulation and other forms of emotional abuse. They will sabotage opportunities. Additionally, the potential to develop emotional and mental disorders become stronger and brain development will be delayed. Other silent contemplations will become pronounced such as, **I AM** worthless, inadequate, unwanted, lonely, undeserving, rejected, angry, inferior and a host of negative emotions all at the same time.

If you are reading this book right now and you can relate to this. THESE ARE ALL LIES!! Please understand that you are NOT a mistake, a failure, or any of the lies that you have believed. God had an intentional plan for your life before the world began. Your parents were just unaware of the intentionality connected to your birth. Please forgive them, if you have not done so already. God knew everything about who you are before you were formed in your mother's womb. He even knew where you would be sitting while reading this book. God has never created a mistake, only masterpieces. Therefore you, my friend, are a masterpiece with a purpose.

After hearing hurtful words over and over again, men and women sometimes believe that something is wrong with them, even if it is a lie. These lies can even douse the passion for life from those with even the greatest confidence. However, I'm convinced that someone telling a lie on us is not the problem. The real problem is when the negative words from others become our self-talk. Negative words from others have an insidious way of making us develop a negative concept of ourselves, if we are not careful. This creates a deficient in self-esteem. Your life will ultimately mirror what you believe about yourself.

I didn't need to hear any of these horrible words from anyone. My self-talk from the trauma of being molested and not having my father present was enough noise. I told myself, **"I am not loveable" and "I am not enough"** because my dad was not there and another individual who was trusted by my family should have protected me, but instead, had decided to molest me. Add to that, the fact that spiritual leaders ignored my cry for help. My being ignored during the most critical time of my life, created additional negative programming. I started to believe **"I didn't have a voice."** Needless to say that I spent a significant amount of time trying to compensate for believing that I was not enough and that I was not being heard. To help you get a picture of what that looked like, here is an example. I always felt an insatiable need to make up for what I thought I was missing. My thoughts created a mindset of scarcity.

I could not take enough showers, and there was not enough Dr. Bronner's peppermint soap in the world that could remove that filthy fingerprint from my body or my soul, so I thought. But, in my own desperate search, I made a new discovery about the mind and brain that only God could have planned. There was no way that I could have come across such a miracle on my own. I discovered how the same mind that experienced disorder would experience order again and still achieve excellence over the long haul.

Neuroscientist and mind-brain experts, Dr. Caroline Leaf and Dr. Shad Helmstetter have jointly conducted more than fifty years of research centered around Neuroplasticity. Neuroplasticity is the amazing capability of the brain to be rewired and restored back to a healthy state. It is by far the greatest brain discovery made. By it, individuals with traumatic brain injuries and those who experience psychological trauma can recover. This discovery further proves that we can truly live the wonderful lives that we were designed to live. Exposure to the truth builds confidence for a greater level of achievement. Exposure is when something that has been hidden and unknown suddenly becomes tangible and within reach. Environments, biology, and birth order have to take a backseat to such revelation. Based on design, any aspect of our lives can change with the amazing power of the brain. In other words, your story can end favorably. Here is how the process starts.

1. **IDENTIFY YOUR AND CONFRONT YOUR LIE.** The only way to solve a problem is to identify it. We all have experienced a traumatic event in our lives, but we have also taken away a different meaning from that event. What have you been telling yourself as a result of an adverse experience? Your answer will expose it. Another question that will expose your lie is, what do I continue to tell myself, ponder and worry about as a result of my past? Keep in mind that your lie may not be something you literally say, but you might harbor the thought and express self-sabotaging behaviors. The only way to move forward into your life effectively is to identity what has been keeping you back for so long and call it a lie.
2. **DETOX FROM THE LIES**. Whenever you are starting afresh, you need a clean slate, so you want to clear out anything that is contrary to the whole truth about who you are. Because this is the start of a major transformation in your life, it's important to get ready for your life’s new trajectory. Liken your identity to the dream home that you want to build. Your first step is not to start building, but to prepare for the dream. Preparation for the dream produces tenacity to maintain the dream. We have to make sure that your new identity is built with the highest quality materials and on land that has been cleared and assessed. So, you

must excavate the land where the house will be built. What this looks like is bulldozing any other structure and cleaning up any debris that may be standing in place of your dream home. In your life, it looks like bull-dozing the lies that have built monuments and the cycles of defeat that have plagued you. Mental, physical and psychological preparation are all required. It may also look like verbally confessing your break-up from the lies that you once believed. Say, "I break every agreement that I've made knowingly or unknowingly with words that are contrary to what God says about me. These words and their effects shall no longer stand in my life. I cut them off by the root."

3. **REPLACE LIES WITH TRUTH**. Now it's time for a new foundation. The important concept to note is that, you can tell your brain what you want it to think. Your brain will respond to your words. The truth and nothing but the truth is what causes change, even though it might hurt at first. Look up scriptures based on what God says about you. There is a specific truth found in the scripture that will offset every individual lie that you have believed. Recognize His Word as the truth. Let truth shape your life. Truth provides a sturdy foundation for you to build your house. And the truth will help you produce better and more positive images of yourself. Use the truth to create the life you want. Use the list of "I AM" statements that I gave earlier. Also use the scriptures that are listed. It's the implanted Word that saves your soul. Remember, these lies are what you have told yourself for your whole life. It will take diligent repetition to replace them. Once the truth populates your heart, your soul and your spirit, you can begin to function successfully and make greater contributions to yourself and the world.

Here are some lies deflected by the Truth! Let the Truth make you free!
Lie: I am made of sugar and spice and everything nice.

Truth: I am the handiwork of God, made in His image and full of His breath (Ephesians 2:10). The Spirit of God created me and the breath of the Almighty has given me life (Job 33:4).
Lie: I can't change.
Truth: God has provided the gift of change and transformation by the renewing of my mind. I am changing into the image of God.
Lie: I can't forgive.
Truth: The power of the Holy Spirit is at work inside of me and enabling me to go beyond my limits. I have the power to forgive because I am forgiven (Ephesians 3:20).
Lie: You are just like your father. You are just like your mother.
Truth: Lord, you have searched me and have known me. I am an individual and you made me uniquely different from anyone else on the planet to fulfill a specific purpose. I am fearfully and wonderfully made (Psalm 139).
Lie: It's my fault.
Truth: I am free from condemnation and Christ is my advocate.
Lie: I am ashamed of who I am.
Truth: I am in right-standing with God, and I am redeemed by the blood of the Lamb.
Lie: I am a mistake.
Truth: God, you had plans for my life to prosper me, even before I was formed in my mother's womb (Jeremiah 1:5). Your eyes have seen my unformed substance, and in the Book of Life are all the days that are appointed for me (Psalm 139:16).
Lie: I will never do anything right.
Truth: I can do all things through Christ who strengthens me (Philippians 4:13).
Lie: I am a failure.
Truth: I am more than a conqueror through Jesus Christ, who loved us (Romans 8:37).

4. **MEDITATE ON YOUR NEW TRUTH.** Meditation on the Word of God is a command and is also a law of prosperity. When meditation is practiced with God as the focus, the words are plastered in our minds and hearts. Eventually, the meditation will materialize. When your

mind opens the door of your spirit, there is a download of wisdom that will feed who you are meant to be, rather than who you have become. Meditation is an intentional practice that promotes healing, revelation, and understanding. I have found that meditation on God's Word helps me to program my thinking so that when I am not meditating, I can automatically bring my thoughts captive to God's Word.

5. **SAY CONFESSIONS AND AFFIRMATIONS DAILY.** God has given each of us a measure of faith, but in order for this measure to mature, it must be fed. There is a principle that says what you feed will live and what you starve will die. Well, this is true for faith as well. Faith comes by repetitiously hearing God's Word. You can take this literally. And guess what? You don't have to be at church to feed your faith. Actually, your brain responds better to your voice than another person's voice. That's why I say daily confessions of the Word of God. I usually take scriptures and create practical, daily declarations that I can say throughout the day. For example: Scripture: Genesis 1:27 reads, "So God created man in His own image, in the image and likeness of God He created him; male and female He created He them."
   Declaration/Confession: Because I was created in the image of God, His character, wisdom, strength and mind were reproduced inside of me.
6. **FLOURISH WITHIN YOUR LIMITATIONS/WEAKNESSES.** Don't worry about who you are not or what you don't have. This may seem strange or invalid, but just like strengths, weaknesses contribute to your success. Knowing them provides an upper hand in understanding the totality of who you are. Being aware of weaknesses also promotes an understanding of how to develop a plan for personal projects and for life. There is no such thing as one-size-fits-all when working on personal development projects, because we all work differently and are stimulated by various factors. Some people are more detailed and others are not as detailed. I fall in the latter

category, and that's okay. My knowing that helps me to set goals and develop plans that support my style of work. On the other hand, my weaknesses help me understand that I need God for everything I do. The same is true in business.

"Unless you were born under a rock, you probably are familiar with the name Crayola. It is the most popular and recognized crayon brand in the world. Every year. Binney & Smith, the company that makes Crayola Products, manufactures nearly 3 billion crayons, at the rate of 12 million a day. That's enough crayons to circle the globe six times.

The company was founded by Joseph Binney in 1864 as the Peekskill Chemical works. In 1885, the founder's son, Edwin, and his cousin, C. Harold Smith, became partners and changed the company's name to Binney & Smith. Up to the turn of the century, the company focused on producing items such as red pigments for barn paint and carbon black used in the making lamp black or automobile tires. And their primary method of product development? Simple: ask customers about their needs and then develop products to meet those needs.

In 1900, the company began making slate pencils for the educational market, and it found that teachers seemed happy to tell company representatives what they desired. When teachers complained about poor chalk, Binney & Smith produced a superior, dustless variety. When they complained that they couldn't buy a decent American Crayon (the best were imported from Europe and very expensive), it developed the Crayola. The company introduced the product to the market in 1903 as a box of eight colors that cost a nickel.

Once the company found its niche in the children's market, it became incredibly focused. For a hundred years, it has manufactured superior art supplies for children. Today it dominates that market-even in the face of electronic revolution. In

the Five Faces of Genesis, Annette Moser-Wellman assessed the company by saying.
"The biggest threat to Crayola's business has been the entry of computer games for kids. Instead of drawing and coloring, kids are tempted by interactive CDs and more. Instead of trying to dominate computer games, Crayola has chosen to flourish within their limitation. They do children's art products better than anyone."

Binney & Smith could have lost focus in an attempt to chase new markets and diversify itself. That's what toy manufacturer Coleco did. The company started out in leather goods in the 1950's and then switched to plastics. In the late 1960s, it was the world's largest manufacturer of above ground swimming pools. It had found its niche. Yet in the 1970s and 1980s, it chased after the computer game market and then low-end computers. (you may remember Coleco Vision) then it tried to capitalize on Cabbage Patch Dolls. This ultimately drove the company into bankruptcy.

It would have been easy for Binny & Smith to chase after other successes, but it did not do that. The company has remained focused. And as long as it does, it will continue to excel and sell more crayons and children's art supplies than any other company in the world. (John Maxwell, Thinking for a Change, 2003 p. 78-79)

This concept is as important in developing yourself, just as it was for this company's sustenance and position as a giant in its industry. It's easy to look at what others are doing and judge yourself unfairly. Your focus on your purpose will give you the advantage and help you to gain better clarity about yourself. You should not feel like something is wrong with you just because you don't have a certain trait or because you may not have a particular strength. Weakness can indeed be as valuable as strength if navigated properly. Look what B&F accomplished by keeping their focus on where they were strong. They made billions by acknowledging where they were weak. Rather than trying to make up for your limitations, find YOUR niche and stay there. Find who you are, your purpose, strengths, gifts, callings and weaknesses and stay there. Allow your weaknesses to help you to navigate and use your strengths. It's okay if you don't know it at the moment, but I'd rather you embark on the process of finding out than trying to be someone you are not. Become who you are designed to be. As long as you are focused on that goal, you will flourish.

When Weakness Works For You

Let's look at a story of a man named Ehud; this was one of the most gruesome stories that I have ever heard, but it will show you how to flourish within your weakness, if your weakness is physical. This story is so gruesome that I still can't believe that it comes from the Bible.

Ehud was hired to perform a scandalous job after his predecessor died. God hired him to kill the king. The people of Israel had disobeyed God again. As usual, they were always doing something they had no business doing, even after God rescued them time and time again. (If I am being honest, this sounds like me sometimes.) This time, they fell into the hands of an evil king named Eglon. Ehud's job was to kill Eglon. The children of Israel were God's favorites, because when they cried out to God for help, God always sent help.

Ehud was a left-handed man. I don't consider that a weakness, but maybe they did during this day. God considered all of Ehud's issues and God still hired him. I'll just float that detail out there as it will become important to the success of his mission. Just flow with me for a moment. The backstory on Ehud is that he was from the tribe of Benjamin. This tribe was full of right-handed swordsmen. Benjamin men were simply born and built for war.

To carry out the mission of killing the king, Ehud had a complicated job ahead of him. He even had to make his own weapon and devise a way to get to the king without being turned away. Ehud's weapon could not resemble anyone else's. Even down to the way the sword was concealed, he needed to set himself up for the win. Again, there was no one-size-fits all; he needed a custom-made sword. He made a 16 to 18-inch sword, strapped it to his right thigh and concealed it under his clothes. Ehud was challenged because he was not exactly built for war like the others from his tribe.

When he'd initially gone to the palace, he did not make it into the king's room. There were too many people around. He would not have been able to get away had he done it on the initial entry. Ehud needed to think of something brilliant in order to appear harmless and innocent. So, he told the guards that he had a secret message to deliver to the king.

Ehud knew that the guards would not check his right thigh if he placed a decoy sword where all of the other "right-handed" Benjamites kept theirs… on the left side. The guards confiscated his decoy weapon, as planned. With the custom dagger still in tact, he entered the castle. The guards escorted Ehud back to the king, only this time, he had the king right where he wanted him—ALONE. The king sent all of his servants away, closing the doors behind them. When the king stood, Ehud did not waste any time. He grabbed the sword from his right thigh and jabbed it into Eglon's stomach. Ehud took off through a side door to the king's chamber and locked it. By the time the guards found Eglon dead, Ehud had already left the city.

The guards overlooked Ehud, just as he planned. Some say he had an advantage. The guards assumed he was weak, yet being left-handed worked in Ehud's favor. Generally, swords are placed on the hip or thigh that is opposite of the dominant hand. Had Ehud been right-handed, the guards would have had reason to check his left side. He was left-handed, which caused the oversight. With regard to Ehud's left-handedness, the next detail is extremely important. The reason Ehud was left-handed was because his right hand was deformed. So, did he really have an advantage? The deformity made his right hand useless. This detail gave the guards no reason to think Ehud would cause any harm. What most would see as a weakness became a strength that helped him to perform his purpose. Not only did Ehud literally destroy a king single-handedly, he was responsible for the freedom of an entire generation.

This whole time, you thought you were weak, but God just wanted to reveal your even greater strengths. He wants you to know that your weaknesses and disabilities are not to make you look or feel bad. They have already been taken into account. Even better, they don't suggest inability. With the magnitude of Ehud's accomplishment, he goes down in history for being one of the greatest warriors of the tribe of Benjamin. Your story could be the same. Your weakness is what you make it. You can allow it to destroy you and make excuses for it or you can take your cue from Ehud and allow God to reveal your strengths. Your weakness could be physical or psychological; you can still be an undefeated warrior. You are not so weak or wrong that God can't use you.

It almost makes no sense to us that God would choose Ehud. That's why God is God. He can take something so seemingly foolish to amaze us into believing and trusting His power. While you see weakness, God sees a warrior. Ehud was only able to get close to the king because he did not deny or hide his weakness. He didn't need to look like anyone else to perform. Had he tried to be right-handed like the others, he would have let his entire generation down. I dare you to be okay with being different. Dare to be different. Remember, this was my mom's anthem.

God does not want you to hide your weakness, even if it's a disability. The very part that you want to hide is what He will use to your advantage. Your enemies and naysayers will wonder how you were able to carry out such a mission. Your co-workers will look in awe at how you climbed the ladder of success with such grace, even with less degrees and experience than them. People will wonder how you were able to come back after that incapacitating addiction and life-threatening experience. It's because God can take something really foolish and use it to confuse those who underestimate, disqualify and overlook you.

Additionally, you were born to be great; a weakness does not change that mandate. It demands that you stay connected to your source: God. By no means, were you created to use weakness as an excuse to remain mediocre or average. Your vulnerability is what can cause you to become favored with those who have the keys to the doors you need to enter. So, don't worry about being underestimated. I know you don't like being underestimated. No one does, but it has its benefits. For Ehud, the guards lessened their security check. They slept on his creativity, wit and mental strength. They forgot he was from a tribe of warriors. For you, maybe people think that because you do not work as fast as others, you are not productive. What they don't know is that you are busy working and making silent strides toward victory. Maybe you need to be underestimated so that people won't see you coming. One thing for certain, by the time they notice you, you will be ahead of the game. Like Ehud, you will already be on to the next project. You will already be performing at your highest. Understand that just because people do not recognize your greatness does not change who you are. Denying a weakness is the only way it can hurt you. Your weakness is not what you thought.

7. **DON'T AGREE**. From now on, when someone says something that you don't agree with, whether it's concerning your identity or your life, I give you permission to verbally disagree with it. TACTFULLY! You don't even need my permission. Remember, this is your life. Don't be afraid of anyone's response. You have to take responsibility for what you allow into your space. My mom is so good at this. One day, we took my grandmother to visit one of her former bosses. He is now using a walker and has had several surgeries due to accidents and age. His health is failing, but he is still mobile and able to get

> around fairly well. It just takes him a while. He was happy to see us when we came. He and my grandmother have been good friends for 50 years. Well, when he saw my mom, they began to talk about life and the path he took to get where he is. In the conversation, my mom said, "You're still looking good, Mr. Bill." He said, "Thank you. I'm old and sick. One day, you're going to be old and in bad shape just like me." Immediately, my mom said "I disagree! No, I am not. That's a lie." She had the right to say it. She did not have to accept anything that she did not want, especially something so negative. I now do the same thing and you should too. Try it.

The foundation of your existence is truth. When foundational work is compromised, breathing can also become difficult and maintaining a structure is almost impossible. You were created by the Almighty and the only TRUE and living God. Never forget that your goal is to reach your potential and be everything that He designed you to be. You are who He says you are. Even though your parents or legal guardians may or may not have meant well, your job is not to critique them now. It's to forgive them and get committed to moving forward with purpose. At this point, you can't live in the past. You can be confident about who you are because you are not a victim of any of the lies that you have been told. Remember, an agreement, whether verbal or written, is a binding contract and has to be broken for its power to be useless. Forget the past by detaching from those lies. Your future is brighter.

CHAPTER 9

What is Your Story?

"There are more people in need of healing than there are hands to do the work of healers."
~Quote inspired by Matthew 9:37

Surely, you have a story to tell. People are waiting to hear it. The problem is that you may shy away from the vulnerability to tell the story. You might also compare your path to others and write off your story and the lessons that you have learned as insignificant. Nothing that you have accomplished, experienced, learned, or overcome is insignificant. Everything has prepared you for now, which is what matters the most. I don't have the most amazing or headline story, nevertheless, I have small but significant moments that created the pages of this book. Even though it may seem like your life has been all over the place and that nothing is connecting, each piece of your life connects to create a beautiful canvas.

I seriously struggled with the confidence to share my story. I told myself that no one would listen because I am not a celebrity. I defeated myself saying, "I don't speak well and I would not be able to hold anyone's attention." I fed myself this inaccurate story for a long time. I was even terrified to write this book. However, I felt called to write it. It became crystal clear that I had a unique message of transformation to share. So, I had to get over the fear and develop the heart to get it done. I had to lean on what was already inside of me so that I did not miss the opportunity to spread healing. Everyday literally became sweeter and I healed my own limiting beliefs by first changing what I told myself. You may not feel ready, because your story might still be developing. As long as you are living, your story will be developing. It never ends. No one really arrives. This is a lifelong journey. Remember when I started writing this book, my story was budding. Every day I added on to it, with the intent that I can share it in a way that inspires you to tell yours. Even though this book will end soon, I am living the pages of this book every day of my life. Breathe Again is my life, not just a book.

There was a very well-known woman in the Bible. Her story encouraged me as I wrote this chapter and reminded me that my being able to obtain anything is cultivated by my own attitude. As much as it may sound like a cliché, attitude really does determine altitude. Attitude can make the person who has experienced the worst level of adversity see themselves as a force to reckon with.

This woman who was known for spending twelve years in and out of doctors' offices and undergoing different treatment programs for a disease that caused a constant flow of blood. She spent a significant amount of money with doctors who promised to cure her, but her condition was not cured, nor did it even improve (Mark 5:26). To exacerbate the ill-managed promises of the doctors, the story even says that the condition grew worse. Can you imagine with me for a moment what it would be like to see doctors for over a decade to treat a disease that caused a constant loss or flow? She did not have the normal flow that usually happens for four to seven days every month... the one that most of us complain about. We even make the people around us suffer with us. She had a constant flow for twelve years. I don't think I want to know what it would be like to have a nonstop menstrual cycle for twelve years. I whine every month as if I did not know that the flow would come, so I definitely couldn't imagine the anguish of bleeding nonstop for twelve years.

This amazing woman, whom we have defined by her issue, didn't just lose blood, but she lost everything that meant anything to her. She lost family, oxygen, strength, circulation and health.

Physical blood only represents one type of loss. The Bible only mentions that she had this one issue of blood, but she most certainly had overall poor health because the blood has many functions. One is to fight off infections and disease. She was losing her power to fight off infections and she could have also been anemic. The myriad of sicknesses that she experienced due to the consistent flow was certainly debilitating, to say the least.

This woman that we affectionately know as the woman with the issue of blood, endured twelve years of physical and emotional pain and suffering. As a result of her being declared unclean, she was isolated for all twelve of the years that she experienced the issue. No one is meant to live in isolation because doing so would be mentally tormenting, not to mention the torment that sickness already causes. Before she became sick, she lived a normal life with family and friends. Upon being labeled as "ceremonially unclean," the normal life was taken from her.

Ceremonially unclean is what they called her. What an insult! Generally, when someone was considered "unclean" in the Bible, they were not good enough (in the eyes of people) to be used by God. They were not seen as worthy. But, who is worthy to be used by God? It's so funny that the disposition of Bible day people parallels the same judgmental disposition we see today. People are quick to disqualify others from the opportunity to advance just because they may not fit into their perfect picture. The pharisaic leaders saw to it that no one advanced if they were not in compliance with their law. Later, the death, burial and resurrection of Jesus Christ would abolish this played out law. By the shedding of His blood, we all become clean.

The Long Loss Road

She lost money. She had seen several doctors who promised they had a cure for her condition. Doctors were capitalizing from her ability to pay them top dollar for treatment. Ironically enough, the treatments were likely more expensive than the visits, plus, her doctors were only prescribing medicine that only caused more problems, as the text expressly states. Ultimately, each treatment caused the woman to spend more money on medications to reverse the problems that another drug had caused. Adding more drugs caused a vicious cycle of poor health. Her money could do nothing for her, not even find proper treatment. No amount of money could replace the losses experienced from her sickness.

She lost her social dignity. She was an outcast. Rejection was an understatement to describe the social disability associated with this issue of blood. This was complete isolation. Because of religious laws, she had to be ostracized publicly, so everyone knew her. Privacy was hard to find, even though she really could not go out. Just think, if this were in our day, she would not be able to show her face to the public without being exposed or marred on social media. "That's her … the unclean lady." It's almost like when someone knows something unfavorable about you, they use that to identify you as if it's your name or a term of endearment. And people are the best at making others feel bad, especially when they are miserable themselves. This could have been the case surrounding this story.

She lost influence. I know several Jewish families. They are pretty wealthy to say the least. They also have influence because money provides a certain level of attention and status. I understand that the woman with the issue of blood was a part of the Jewish culture, so she came from wealth. This provided a certain level of influence for her. People looked up to her, prior to her illness.

She lost her family and friends. I understand that this amazing woman was married and even had children. She was raising a family. Mothers take pride in being able to nurture their families by cooking, bonding and sharing experiences that would shape life. She couldn't. Societal laws almost seemed like Jim Crow Laws. They banned her from places for something beyond her control. Imagine the same rules staring her in the face at home.

How could she be proud to be a woman? Imagine not being able to wrap your arms around your children or other family members.

She lost self-esteem. Her self-esteem was likely very poor because she internalized being rejected. She had no one to talk to. Certainly, she was not able to live abundantly because one of the requirements for a fulfilling life is positive self-esteem. With the rejection she received, maybe she felt suicidal. The religious laws of that time made her feel unworthy. Society gave her degrading labels. Anything she touched was suddenly considered dirty. Anything she sat on or laid on had to be washed or burned. One thing that I know about self-esteem is that it is fueled by how we view ourselves, but constantly hearing her name in a negative way, plus being treated horribly caused her to adopt these thoughts of herself. Imagine turning on the news or picking up your phone and seeing articles that degraded who you are.

This legendary woman, who was not even given a name in the Bible, exudes what it means to persevere. Thousands of years later, her story is used to transform lives, in addition to facilitating mental and physical healing as well as deliverance to people, especially women all around the world. This story, just like many other stories in the Bible, shows that faith in God has the ability to accomplish things that ignore logic. We call them miracles. Most of us would have shattered due to the social, financial, emotional and mental strain. I have to be honest with you for a moment and say digging into the details of this story caused a great level of concern on my part. To be publicly marred for something that I could not control would literally poke holes in my emotional health and cause my self-esteem to decline.

Like you, I have definitely had hurtful experiences that gained public attention. It wasn't at this capacity, but I have definitely had some humiliating moments. Maybe you were hurt at a church, a job or another organization where leaders abused their authority. You may have experienced a public hurtful break-up, your reputation could have been poor due to bad decisions, you may have been fired or you may be currently fighting with an illness. Some way or another, trials come without our permission. And we all process experiences differently. However, we can definitely take a cue from this amazing story of endurance. No matter what your experience is, Jesus shows His compassion to you through your active display of faith. Although this issue was likely biological in origin, I believe that in order for the woman to receive wholeness, she had to allow the truth of God's Word to renew her mind. Truth says that she is not a victim of her biology or her environment. Without the renewing of her mind, she would have stayed in the house when she saw Jesus passing through the town. Logic would have destroyed her faith.

The Miracle

Growing up in a Jewish household, she was taught from the Torah, a very specific part of the Bible that Jews use to become versed in who God is, as well as gain knowledge of His principles. So, she was trained in spiritual concepts. She had a mature understanding of God's Word. In the Jewish traditions, parents began diligently teaching their children as soon as they are able to walk and talk. She was no baby when it came to her knowledge of God, His laws and His supernatural ability. The knowledge that she'd received as a child sparked her eagerness to want God to reveal Himself to her as the Jehovah Rapha that she'd read and studied about over the years. By the time we are introduced to her in the fifth chapter of Mark, she was ready to do anything to meet this God in the flesh. Even if that meant putting herself at risk to be killed by religious, pharisaic leaders, because she was not supposed to go near or touch anyone. She would technically make Jesus unclean. Pharisees were looking for a reason to kill or disqualify anyone.

This brave woman heard that Jesus was in her town. She made her mind up to leave the house and go meet Him. Had she considered logic or rules, she would have disqualified herself and missed the opportunity of a lifetime. I'm sure that every thought she had was opposing her decision. And for her to get through such a rambunctious crowd, she had to be either desperate or out of her mind. As she was pressing her way through the crowd, she was pressing her way through twelve years of agony, torment and, disability. She could have given up and died, but she pushed through with perseverance. The key to this woman's success was the exact definition of vision-thinking outside of where she was. One moment of faith was able to overturn over a decade of agony, every ill-managed promise from doctors, every idle word spoken, every dime she'd lost and, every day of heartache.

Mark 5:28 (AMP) says, "For she ***thought,*** If I just touch his clothing, I will get well." This says to me she'd won the battle in her mind. Remember that if anything touched her, according to the law, that thing was now unclean. She was taking her cue from the very Jesus she was getting ready to touch. He was a rule breaker (in a good way), and she was about to break a rule. Society put a label on her because she'd bled for so long. This is similar to the way that society will label you. I'm one who believes that rules can be broken as long as they are broken with purpose. Jesus healed on the Sabbath day and He also did things like claim Himself to be the Son of God. Both of these broke the rules, but they served a great purpose. And lives were transformed as a result.

Upon beginning the journey to see Jesus, she had to begin renewing her mind or detoxing it from all the twelve years of disappointing, defeated thoughts of hopelessness. She could have closed the book on her life's story but faith told her the plot could change. Her thought was being operated on by faith and her faith was being activated by the teachings that she'd received when she was growing up. In an instant, at the sight of Jesus, she was able to recall the faith of her childhood. She began to replace old thoughts with the Word that she knew. I believe that her faith literally came by hearing the Word of God so much as a child. The moment she needed it, she was able to access it.

So, she really displayed what it means to be led by faith. When the woman's faith guided her to Jesus, she touched Him and was immediately healed of the distressing ailment. Although she was healed immediately, she fell to the ground in fear and began to pour out her heart to Jesus. And He listened. For twelve years, she had been avoided and denied hugs, handshakes and other common social norms, but in a moment's time, Jesus listened to her attentively to find out her issue. He compassionately said, "Your faith has made you whole. Go in peace and be continually healed and freed from your disease" (Mark 5:34 AMP).

In a moment, God healed, increased faith, restored hope and renewed mental health. The power that God has given us in our minds is so amazing. We are all candidates for having our minds renewed and to get our thinking in alignment with God's Word. Renewed thinking is vital to a successful life. PERIOD.

How to Renew Your Mind

For the majority of my life, most of my thoughts were negative. I had encountered so many domestic disappointments that I doubted if anything really good could happen. Coupled with that, exposing my heart to toxic situations disrupted my thoughts. The statement, "You are what you eat," is true, but not only for natural food, it's also true for consumption on any level. I had never really grasped the understanding of how phenomenal God created my mind to be. I had never considered monitoring my thoughts until I began to see the physical symptoms of my negative thought patterns, such as panic attacks, loss of appetite, hair loss from stress, brain fog, sleep deprivation and the list goes on.

By using the power of the mind, everything that opposes our peace can be defeated and we can have victory over such a poor mental attitude. I believe a healthy mindset can be accomplished if we use the power that we have been given to transform our thinking.

"And be not conformed to this world: but be ye transformed by the renewing of your mind, that ye may prove what is that good, and acceptable, and perfect, will of God." Romans 12:2

Success is inner work. This is what Paul was telling the Romans. Old paradigms of thinking will not get you to the next level. Renewing your mind will literally transform your life. By virtue of the way we were built to think, we can transform our thinking in a way that helps us to reflect good thoughts, which will help us to achieve good lives. But we just have to be intentional and diligent to the process. Even after years of negative thinking and disappointments, loss, and misfortunes, we have been given an amazing capacity to transform our lives by renewing our minds daily. God has provided instructions for your success. They are:

1. Learn what God's thoughts towards you are through His Word. Become diligent to learn what He says about you and establish your findings as truth. God's Word will repopulate your mind and the old negative thoughts will be replaced by positive thoughts. This process has to be a commitment as thoughts are forever flowing and can be influenced by exposure. God's Word refines, causes a new mindset to form and becomes food for your soul.

1.

"Finally, brethren, whatsoever things are true, whatsoever things are honest, whatsoever things are just, whatsoever things are pure, whatsoever things are lovely, whatsoever things are of good report; if there be any virtue, and if there be any praise, think on these things". Philippians 4:8

2. Meditate on the Word of God. There has been some controversy in the world at large around the practice of meditation and whether or not "Christians" should meditate. Meditation is not tied to a particular religion. However, what you meditate on makes the difference. We are commanded to meditate because of the many benefits, such as concentration, focus, insight, revelation and prosperity. David, in the Bible, made meditation a habit when he was going through the storms he recorded in the Book of Psalms. He became victorious. We meditate on the Word of God so that the Word can become implanted in our thoughts. The foundation of our success in life is given in Joshua 1:8.

"This book of the law shall not depart from your mouth, but you shall read [and meditate on] it day and night, so that you may be careful to do [everything] in accordance with all that is written in it; for then you will make your way prosperous and you then will be successful." Joshua 1:8

Meditation played a big role in my victory over depression. I needed a way to gain control over my past life of undisciplined thoughts. My meditation practice helped me become aware of my thoughts and to ultimately gain control over them. When I first started meditation, I always used a guided meditation where I was led step-by-step. But now, I can choose a phrase, a scripture or a thought and sit in a still, comfortable position for seven to ten minutes breathing deeply. I usually play instrumental music in the background with the sounds of nature. I use that time to rehearse the phrase over and over in my head. Not in an attempt to cancel my mind, but to tell my mind what I want it to think. You don't have to try to cancel your mind, you can gain control of it. When an erroneous thought invades my mind during meditation, I bring my focus back to my breath and continue this process over and over for the duration of the time. The practice of meditation will help you become more aware of what is entering your mind. During the practice of meditation, your focus is on one particular subject, concept or verse. Sometimes, I just focus on my breathing.

3. Use the Word as a weapon in your prayer. People used to say, "Sticks and stones may break my bones, but words will never hurt me." Don't believe it. It's another one of those lies. This is a really silly way to teach children not to respond to other children that tease them with their words. But, there is no validity behind this statement, and it is causing more harm than help. Words are literal weapons that have the power to pierce, kill and demean. Although we are not fighting the people who sometimes seem as if they are our enemies, we must stay covered in the whole armor of God, because He has given us weapons for the wars that we face. The true enemy is unseen. God's Word is actually the most incorruptible spiritual weapon that God gives us permission to use when fighting our enemy.

You will put the enemy to shame when you use the Word of God against him as arrows and missiles in prayer. Remember, it was God's Word that defeated the enemy in the Bible days, and today, the same truth stands. The Word works every time. We can't be passive with this fight. These are our lives we're defending. The combination of prayer and God's Word is more powerful still. Prayer using God's Word activates to release the promises of God into our lives daily. In moments of warfare, or if you need an uplifting word to help a friend, you might not have time to go find your Bible. I encourage the study and memorization of God's Word, so that in the moment of demand, the Holy Spirit will help you to recall the scripture that you will use. And as we live in God and allow His Word to become a part of our lives, we can pray more confidently, throwing death blows at the real enemy.

4. Practice Mindfulness. That is, practice staying aware of your minute-by-minute thoughts. Overall, it keeps your mind attentive of its mental activity. Although every thought should not be trusted, nothing should enter your mental space without your noticing it. In biblical terms, we refer to this as taking every thought captive. "We are created with the skill to bring thoughts captive."~Dr. Caroline Leaf. However, this is the hardest task to do if it has not been practiced, yet the most important. Mindfulness will help you decide what thoughts are yours and should be practiced and what should be trashed.

5. Don't Quit. I know we live in a popcorn generation and we want everything to be quick, but gaining control of your thought-life will actually take time. Essentially, you are breaking habits of old thinking patterns that it took you years to develop, so it will take time to break! If you are thinking about God's Word as a seed, remember that agricultural law, which is also true in the spiritual world of sowing and reaping, says that just as you plant a seed, there is a WAITING period between the planting and the harvesting. The same is true for the Word of God being planted into your spirit. You must water the seed with prayer and meditation and patiently expect the harvest to be plentiful.

Twelve years of a long-standing illness and enduring the judgments of irresponsible people were forever changed in one moment of faith a moment that allowed the woman with the issue of blood to become a legend. Fight back against what you have been told and see yourself in the truth. Let your determination reflect the determination of this courageous woman. She didn't even have a name in the Bible, but she will never be forgotten.

She was metaphorically walking through fire, but God was with her. He will also be with you. You have a story. The details might not be like the woman with the issue of blood. No matter the magnitude, it will heal and inspire others. We often think that the good stories help others, but it's the failures, the struggles and the mess that qualify us to heal the world. How can someone who has only experienced bliss help those who have lived on the rough side of the tracks? Your story may not be what you want it to be yet. You can change the dynamics. Take people on the journey from where you were to your current location and keep working towards the desired outcome. Tell your story, no matter what phase of the story you are in! Your story will be told by people and used as the synopsis to promote restoration. It's your struggle and your resilience that will keep your name from being erased from history. The world is waiting to hear it.

CHAPTER 10

The R.E.A.L. You

(Righteous, Esteemed, Accepted, Loved)

"What good would it do to get everything you want and lose you, the real you"
Mark 8:36 [MSG]

"That's me!" or "I'm her," is what little girls say when they see a popular singer, actress or model on television, wrapped in the conventional standard of beauty. The admiration from a seemingly safe virtual distance then becomes an attempt to mimic the personality of the celebrity in day-to-day life. Knowingly or unknowingly, we have seen this play out right under our noses, especially when we tried to become the star. I believe this behavior subconsciously contributes to the mindset that conventional body and beauty are more significant than purpose.

Later on, it dawns on us that these same people who we see as role models, even those who don't fit the bill of conventional beauty, do not overemphasize their looks. Not all, but some. We often notice their beauty more than they do. They view their looks as less important than their performance or their ability to capture their fans. When we have trouble seeing what we are good at, we try to become the socially accepted definition of cool, even if it's not authentic, sometimes, to our detriment. If it's so much fun to be a celebrity, why don't all celebrities think so? I could never imagine the day that I would work, trying to be like a person who had the same imperfections as me, but had better acting skills to hide those imperfections.

Maybe you have been that little girl or witnessed another girl mesmerized by that image. Either way, the reason is socially motivated. We live in a day and age where everything is characterized by stress and pressure to measure up to what looks good. People are running around in confusion for treasures they have within. As a result of a negative self-concept, they are doubtful and often shy away from their REAL identities. This is comparison at its best.

Although comparison is not ideal in the long-run, it can help us if we let it. The need to compare reveals that there is untapped inner greatness that is seeking expression, howbeit, it has not yet met the eye. However, we have been addressing it the wrong way. The problem with comparison is not that it's characterized by an attraction to something or someone that may look or seem to be better. There is nothing wrong with noticing that someone is better in skill, productivity and intellect, yet worthy of the same respect. We need people around us who are better, so that we are challenged to become better. We must use our observation in terms of becoming better at who we are supposed to be, rather than as an invitation to mimic another person.

The problem is that comparison is characterized by thoughts that say, "That's what I'm missing," "I'm not enough," or "I'm less than." In other words, your sense of self has been developed from a place of lack. It's all in your mind and this way of reasoning causes the primitive brain to work. Only a mentality of lack questions its value and struggles to produce authentically.

Since we live in the world of social media, let's use those examples. To see someone who is traveling to exotic locations, looking confident, working out, and happily married may cause feelings of insecurity to surface, especially if your life does not mirror that person's life. All too often, we fail to consider that none of what we perceive as that person's "advantages" made the person happy, that is, IF he or she is really happy. Additionally, when we look at a person that we are comparing ourselves to, we only see from one vantage point. This vantage point does not provide the full story of that person's life. Contrary to what some say, pictures do lie. You may not always be looking at better. If you are viewing someone's life from a place of brokenness and do not know who you are, any vacation or marriage will look better. What they are selling you is that vacations, marriage, outgoing and confident pictures equate to happiness. This is not always the case. I'm not saying that everyone on social media is faking, but some people are. Still, your goal is not to mimic another person's joy. The goal is to figure out what will bring you the fulfillment and satisfaction that you are looking for and aggressively go after that.

Social media has become the standard as people gauge their worth by how many likes they receive on any given post. The condition of the heart responsible for posting is seeking love, worth and belonging. W settles for a "like" here and there because we have not discovered that the first love comes from God and self. God's love provokes us to love ourselves and change our self-concepts to reflect His love. If we become self-aware and take the time to understand the innate treasures of our true selves, we can set standards based on our assignments and callings, and what we authentically want, rather than from pictures we've captured just to appear a certain way. And we can really take control of our lives. I want to be clear that when I say take control of your life, I don't mean trying to take God's place. I mean managing the measure that God gives you.

When we are aware of our identities in Christ, Satan is limited in his enterprise against us. We can spread the good news that Jesus brings, the world will be healed, we can really live the lives that we should live as kings and queens, and we can literally bring Heaven to Earth. We set ourselves up for hardship when we don't live in alignment with His plans and purpose for authority and when we don't embrace our own unique way of being. Kingdom living should not have to be something we look forward to upon our transitions from this life. We should expect it NOW.

God will not place dreams in our hearts if He does not plan to bring them to pass while we are living.

What Are You Telling Yourself?

Your beliefs expressly flow out of your mouth, no matter how you try to avoid it. And your thoughts are talking to your brain even if you choose not to open your mouth. Your self-talk is important. The woman who can believe that God is who He says He is, is living her best life in real life, not just on social media. She tells herself, "I was created to live authentically and abundantly, and I will accept nothing less." Another woman may believe that she has nothing to offer and will continue to say things that prove her beliefs. Dr. Caroline Leaf contends that as you are thinking and making decisions mentally, you influence your genetic expression and build your interpretation of who you think you are into a physical display. I interpret this to mean that whatever I think about over an extended period of time will eventually begin to take form in my life tangibly. You have been designed for a healthy way of thinking because God gave you His mind. You can use the amazing power of your mind to live a great life.

The Fall of Adam

We started the book understanding our creation, as recorded in the first few chapters of Genesis. As I consider the fall of Adam and its consequences for mankind, I see how the fall was in perfect alignment with God's plan to call man back into proper positioning. What seemed like a curse was actually God at work. This is a true example of a crisis turned into an opportunity. Some people will blame Adam, but I appreciate him at the same time, because Jesus did His best work for our resurgence and our uprising. Just like God used the struggle of Adam to do a great work, He can do the same with your struggles and faults. Your struggles can literally be used as stepping-stones that help you to reach your high calling. Your high calling is equivalent to the pinnacles of success that you dream about. I believe that, for some reason, God preserved the uprising of women for this very moment we're living in. Historically, the achievements of women went under the radar and had to be dug up so that we could learn the truth about our history and heritage. Nowadays, women can't be hidden, as we appear on the covers of major magazines and are highlighted across world news outlets. Women are really making consistent strides so that our names and achievements will not be obliterated from history.

Identity vs. Behavior

Most people would believe the theoretical idea that behavior determines identity. The crucial truth is that when identity is established, behavior is determined and influenced by the knowledge and understanding of identity. We are ultimately held captive and will operate according to the truth that we believe about ourselves. In other words, self-discovery can help us all make connections and discoveries about why we may respond a certain way, why we like and dislike things and why we have certain proclivities or leanings toward others. Consequently, whatever we know and believe about ourselves is reflected in every other area of our lives. Therefore, if our truth is skewed, our lives are skewed. For this reason, I believe that we must begin to show people who they really are, empower them with knowledge of their REAL identities and stop addressing them based on their behavior. Addressing a person based on his or her negative attributes will always warrant an undignified response. What did Jesus do when the woman had an infirmity? He did not point out the obvious by telling her that she was sick. He already knew that and so did she. For what other reason would she have been looking for Him? He spoke in the affirmative. He reminded her that she was healed and said, "Woman, thou art loosed." He spoke into her spirit, and everything dead was revived. The same grace must be extended as an approach to those who have made wrong decisions and those who are ill. We can't be judgmental or insensitive. We must relate and have the heart of Jesus for people. He was moved with compassion, not judgment and condemnation (John 3:17). He loved the person, but hated the sin. Without constantly reminding a person of their sin, we can tell them who they are; this approach will help them to make the connection between their identity and their behavior. Revelation of identity has life-changing power.

*"But the people that do **know** their God shall **be** strong and **do** great exploits"~Daniel 11:32*

I believe compassion is especially needed in the church at large or any other entity that influences the well-being of humanity. So many people go to church for years, and before they are convinced that God even loves them, they are told how they need to behave and made aware of all of the behaviors that God does not accept. You know the human brain does not process negatives very well. It has been psychologically proven that when the mind hears negative words in a statement, that sentence can throw the brain off, making it more difficult to understand. We are better off when we are told what we can do, rather than what we can't, and who we are, rather than who we are not.

I once read a story about a man who was raised fatherless. He was born without even knowing who his father was. Fatherlessness has always been a great source of shame. I especially see how it could be demeaning in a small town where everybody knows everybody. As a boy, he had never gone to church, but one Sunday, he decided to go hear the new pastor of a local church preach. Even as a boy who had not experienced church, he thought the new guy was pretty good … so good that the little "illegitimate" boy went back again and again. In fact, he started to attend every Sunday. His shame from being a bastard child in the literal sense of the word went with him. Due to his shame, he always arrived on time enough to hear the preacher and he left early … all to avoid talking to people and being looked at by anyone. Well, on one particular Sunday, he got so engaged and caught up in the service that the unthinkable happened. He forgot to leave early. Before he knew it, the final prayer had been prayed and the service was over. People began to fill the aisles to file out of the church. There he was between the rows waiting for the opportunity to leave without being noticed. When his time came, he took a mad dash to the door, rushing past crowds of people. As he got closer to the door, he felt a heavy hand land on his shoulder. He turned around and looked up to find the preacher looking down at him asking,

"What is your name, boy? Whose son are you?"

The little boy died inside. The very thing that he feared and had tried to avoid was in his face, confronting him. Before he could say anything, the preacher said,

"Wait. I know who you are and I know who your family is. There is a distinct family resemblance."

"You do?" the boy asked.

"Why yes, I do. YOU ARE THE SON... YOU'RE THE SON OF ... YOU ARE THE SON OF GOD!"

From that day onward, the boy was never late to church again and he made it his responsibility to speak to the pastor and a few others on the way out of the door. (*It's Friday but Sunday's Coming:* Word, 1985)

Those words changed his life forever. As you can see from the story, years of shame from being a fatherless child were all obliterated by the simple revelation of identity. The experience of unrelenting disappointment weighed heavily on the boy's well-being to the point that he left church early to avoid having to face the shame. His heart was sick, but by way of a divine encounter with the preacher, his life changed. Over the course of his life, no one had ever called him who he REALLY was. The people of the community probably identified him as a bastard child. In return, he identified right back with being the bastard child. He likely thought, "I am indeed a bastard child, so I should be addressed as such." That was his self-talk until the day a sudden good break turned his entire life around. The preacher made him aware of a new truth... a truth that did not mirror what everyone else in his past had said of him. "You are the son of God." Those words brought hope to his hopeless heart. Truth has the power to overcome facts on any day of the week. I believe his faith was increased to grow up not thinking about the facts, but to be fortified by the Word of Truth. It was a simple and concise but powerful statement that ignited a fire in him … a positive encounter destroyed every negative thought or opinion that had ever been echoed. All it took was one simple word of truth from God to heal his weary heart. I believe that revelation destroyed generations of curses that could have been held over every child in his family, even those unborn. Finding out that he is really the son of God gave his life new meaning. His natural birth and natural existence did not exist in that moment. The spirit was magnified over the natural. And spiritual identity trumps the natural on any day of the week.

Similar to the story, your biggest challenge has been ignorance of who you are. The REAL you will require you to stop believing the lies. Satan, who works with the enemy inside your head, has been forcefully using your ignorance against you. Such vehemence is only an indication that the REAL you is so extraordinarily powerful that he had to throw everything in your path that would keep you in the dark, separated from your bright future. He knows that if you are struggling to breathe, you will struggle to do everything else. He knows better than you do that you are a force that can't be stopped. He will even use natural facts against you until you start using them against yourself. The same way he did to me, the "bastard child" and countless others. No matter what your natural situation is, your Father God numbered the hairs on your head and you are the apple of His eye. If it had not been for the obstacles that you faced and the perplexities, you would not have the grit or the desire to be more than you are and to slay every Goliath that comes your way. Understand that your mistakes don't intimidate Him, your stubbornness does not scare Him, and neither does your sin. He conquered all of the above. So, how much more can He do with you? Give God, your real Father, the opportunity to use you, mold you and make you into the fearless, bold, intrepid, REAL woman that He created you to be.

Who is the REAL You?

The problem is that everybody is claiming to be REAL, but there is really no consensus on what being REAL looks like. The knowledge of the REAL you is a breakthrough revelation. It provides an anchor to hang onto when you are hedged and pressed into a corner, troubled and oppressed in every way. When you can suffer embarrassments, relationship failures, failures in business, and the perplexities of life, the REAL you won't let you or anyone else drive you into despair. During times of being pursued and persecuted, the REAL you confirms that you are not alone and that your persecution has a great reward; you are still undefeated. When you are stricken down by life's circumstances, the REAL you will not be destroyed.

"We are troubled on every side, but not distressed; we are perplexed, but not in despair; Persecuted, but not forsaken; cast down, but not destroyed." 2 Corinthians 4:8-9).

The REAL you is a combination of elements. It's who you are at the soul level. It is the foundation of your existence: your original way of thinking, showing emotions, and being. The REAL you is who you are at your core without considering titles, physical attributes, bank accounts, where you fall on the organizational chart, degrees or associations. It is the ORGANIC you. No GMOs. We are not talking about food, but you get it. The REAL you shows total confidence in who you are and why you were created. The REAL you can defy the odds that are stacked against you. The REAL you is knowing that you were made in the image of God and operating in the authority and power that comes with it. The REAL you is focused on your God-given mission to destroy the works of darkness. The REAL you does not play small to satisfy others. The REAL you walks tall and confident, no matter what. The REAL you finds hope in hopeless situations. You are called to success and this requires the ability to navigate adversity. The REAL you knows that you are unique and does not allow anyone or anything to threaten that uniqueness. The REAL you does not compare yourself to others. The REAL you can ask for what you want without fear of rejection. The REAL you knows your worth and does not give discounts. The REAL you does not apologize for prospering. The REAL you is intrepid in your pursuit of purpose.

The REAL you is the person who is authentically and fully settled in her identity in Christ; the REAL you is winning this journey called life. The REAL You demands that you fire the primitive desire for what is—easy. You are called to success and it requires the ability to navigate adversity.

From a spiritual perspective, The REAL you is based on four biblical truths concerning identity. REAL is an acronym that stands for Righteous, Esteemed, Accepted and Loved. REAL represents attributes that you have simply because you were made in the image of God and you are His child. Being REAL does not change based on socioeconomic status, fame, biology, birth order, sociology, credentials, titles or any of the things that we think make up our identities. Your identity is TRUTH. Because it's not based on anything that you can do or what you have done, but what our Father has done. If the truth is you are righteous, esteemed, accepted and loved, amongst many other accolades, it goes without saying that we have the responsibility of aligning our lives with our truth. Any other contrary ideas are lies and illusions that have gained legality through agreements, decisions and memories. You have a moral obligation to be your best self, which is the REAL you. I hate to give it to you like this, but I love you too much to sugarcoat the truth. You are my sister and I am my sister's keeper. You have been given permission to play the victim and make excuses for yourself for too long. You may have been victimized before, just like you may have failed before, but this does not make you a victim or a failure. The dominating, resilient, courageous, REAL you, is ready to be exposed. She will not be exposed without making strategic decisions. I have had to think my way out of agony. LITERALLY! So, it can be done. Doing so has allowed me to create a completely new outlook. And guess what? I used what was already inside of me. When the REAL you is unlocked, the impostor has to leave. REAL and fake can't occupy the same space simultaneously. The REAL you was sealed the minute you accepted Christ as your Lord and Savior (Ephesians 1:13). No one can change what has been sealed and settled by the Holy Spirit.

I AM GOD'S RIGHTEOUS

What Is Righteousness?

Righteousness is a gift that allows you and me to stand before God and be seen as Jesus, the only one without sin. This means we get the opportunity to reap the benefits of Jesus without ever experiencing the agony that He experienced. Learning this changed my life before my eyes. I literally heard the sound of chains falling off of my life; I felt heaviness leaving. My breathing became rhythmic to match the pace of God's love, giving me a life worth living. I felt like a person coming home after being in prison for years. I felt like my life was waiting for this very moment. I had been living in a Christian straight jacket the whole time. The truth really did make me FREE! Not free to do what we want to do, according to my sinful desires. Instead, it provides freedom, power and grace to act in accordance with God's plan.

"It was for this freedom that Christ set us free [completely liberating us]; therefore keep standing firm and do not be subject again to a yoke of slavery [which you once removed]." Galatians 5:1 AMP

Jesus is without sin. That's exactly how God sees you when you accept His Son, Jesus Christ, into your life. PAUSE: if you have not accepted Christ into your heart, NOW is the perfect time. Please pray this with me.

"Father, I first want to thank you for being open and hearing my prayer. For too long, I have kept you out of my life, trying to do my own thing. No longer will I shut you out until I need you. Father, I ask that you reveal your plan to me and help me live my life according to your perfect plan. God, I ask that you would forgive me for trying to save myself. Restore my trust in you so that I can receive your grace and all that your death, burial, and resurrection accomplished. I believe that I am ready to trust you as my Lord and Savior. I believe that you came to Earth, died for my sins, sickness and sorrows. You also rose again so that I can live my best life. Now that I am saved, please send your Holy

Spirit to help, teach, counsel, lead, control and develop me so that I can do your will for the rest of my life. In the name of Jesus I pray. AMEN."

REJOICE! This prayer alone is one of the most important prayers that you will ever pray. Not only are you righteous, you are now forgiven, healed, protected, loved and graced by God. Here is what just happened when you prayed. According to Romans 5:19, which says, "For as by one man's disobedience many were made sinners. So by the obedience of one shall many be made righteous". So, let's say hypothetically that you are 35 and have never been to church, you practiced a religion outside of Christianity for your entire life and you hadn't believed in Jesus before now. The wonderful news is you still became righteous after saying that prayer. This may be hard for you to believe, but it's true. The same way that we gain the sinner's nature by simply being born, we have the nature of righteousness by simply being born again. The prayer you just prayed made that possible. We were ALL born into sin because of Adam and then born AGAIN into righteousness because of Christ. So, the blessing is that you can trash your list of rules. Rules do nothing but cause more pain and shame once violated. The work has been done for you. The only reason that you can even approach the Father is because of what Jesus did. Hence, the reason we pray, "Father, in the name of Jesus," not "Father, in my name." Our name holds no weight when it comes to righteousness. I always scratch my head when people throw their names around as if they died for the world. There is only ONE name that will save us. The name is Jesus! He died for all of us, not just for a chosen group. Most importantly, He died in our place as the Bible declares that Jesus became sin. He stands in our place before His Father. When God looks at us, He sees Jesus. You are made righteous by the obedience of Jesus Christ. I'm not justifying sinful behavior, but I am saying that condemnation has no power because you've been redeemed.
Dr. Creflo Dollar says it this way…

"The day you got born again and made Jesus the Lord of your life, you were made the righteousness of God because of what

you believe. That day, God declared you righteous. Your righteous lifestyle does not produce righteousness, but righteousness will produce a righteous lifestyle." ~Dr. Creflo Dollar

Although, I grew up in the church, my definition of righteousness was completely wrong. For so long, I allowed religion to shape my behavior, which never yields happy results. Consequently, when I imagined being righteous, I subconsciously based it on behavior. If it were about behavior, we would all be disqualified from righteousness. My thought was, "I can't do righteousness! I'm not good enough, disciplined enough, smart enough or dedicated enough." But, I still had my list of rules in my desperate attempt to achieve it on my own. And I still sinned. Like you may have, I defeated myself before I even knew what it really was. That's why spiritual leaders must do an exceptional job teaching people real biblical principles and terminology. We must also take the time to seek understanding of God's Word. Many of the concepts that we grew up believing are not biblical. While they may have some truth, they are based on our own definitions and experiences. As a result, we have forced ourselves into a paradigm that has no validity. Some concepts have been identified as religious dogma because they drive people to seek freedom from a distorted meaning of righteousness. What I learned is that in my striving for the perfect Christian persona, I forfeited the real power that was available to me from the beginning.

Striving to be righteous in my own strength made me become extremely judgmental of others. I was living a double life. On the weekends, I was at the strip club, smoking weed, and drinking. I was steadily pointing my finger and judging the Christians who had my secret sins. How religious! Although we should live in a way that reflects mature behavior and gratitude for our salvation, behavior does not determine righteousness. Righteousness is a grace gift that has been GIVEN to us. Going for broke does not help us achieve such gift.

Letting Go of Perfection

Are you one of those people who attempts to produce flawless work and perfect image? Perfection is impossible but creeps into our nature and becomes an unspoken self expectation. Perfect is a word that has many definitions. Out of all the definitions, we extract the meaning, "to be without flaw" and unfairly determine that our lives must match this definition. Perfect also means good enough, complete, growing, maturing, developing and progressing closer to God. There is a tendency to think that we can only be the one definition of perfect. Yet, we will not apply the healthy meaning of perfect to our lives. Obviously, no one meets the first definition of perfect, but if we harness the latter definition, which is a function of our identities, we can live assured that we are indeed good enough.

I want to ask you another question. **Do you have the courage to let go of the unhealthy definition of perfect?** If perfection has become your mode of operation, the task may be a lot to ask from you, but still, I ask. Are you ready to say bye to perfection?

REAL life is far from being flawless. God knows that so He will never set you up for failure. Failure is not bad, but this type of failure becomes seemingly impossible to recover from because it becomes a cycle. Excellence and progress as the goal create the capacity to grow from failures and continue to work towards success. Maturation allows you to embrace the process, rather than performing for vain expectations of people. The other goal is to have an impact on people. Having an impact while trying to be perfect is impossible. Trying to make progress and be perfect is also impossible. They are both as impossible as trying to walk forward and backward at the same time. YOU CAN'T.
Hence, perfectionism is killing your creativity, productivity and burning you out at the same time. True progress is hitting goals, reaching deadlines and completing projects. Perfectionism won't allow that. Only when you stop trying to be perfect can you tap into the REAL you and operate as your best self.

We live in the dispensation of grace which is God's enabling power. From this position of authority, we are revived back to life. Receiving grace helps us to adjust our behavior to match our identities. If we don't accept God's love and grace, the tendency to be deceived by poor behavior will have an adverse effect. "I am what I did" or "I am my past" will be the ongoing thoughts behind every poor choice. Rather than feeling graced, you will feel void of grace based on your poor performance. Perhaps, your behavior has left something to be desired because you have been striving to "*do*" before being clear about who you are or what Jesus did for you.

I know this may be uncomfortable to hear because it pushes against what has become normal. And some of us have been in the wrong position for so long that we feel the discomfort of the change taking place. Almost like having braces, getting the braces tightened is torture. The pain comes from the braces repositioning and correcting crooked teeth, after being incorrectly positioned for so long. The results are life changing, but the process is sometimes grueling.

So, the litmus test for being counted as righteous is not how well your behavior is or how well you can perform. We can all take a bow if it's based on performance. This was GIFTED to you when you gave your life to the Lord. Righteousness is a position of identity.
Under the umbrella of righteousness, you are redeemed, forgiven and free from shame and condemnation.

REDEEMED

When I was growing up, we used to say, "Can I have a do-over?" when we failed or did something wrong, especially if it was in front of our friends. We were simply asking for a chance to prove that we can do a better job. Quite naturally, we want to leave our best impression. Asking for a "do-over" is the same as wanting to redeem yourself. I can't speak for you, but I have wanted to redeem myself several times in my life. I remember when I completely blew my entire performance in a church play. It was horrible. I have also asked to retake tests that I have completely bombed. Have you been there? If you have, I have good news. This concept does not translate into your new life; it's actually the complete opposite.

Since you are now saved, you are unable to do anything that is so bad that it can change the TRUTH concerning your redemption and your identity. Even better than that, you don't have to redeem yourself at all. Ask for forgiveness, and by God's grace, you have already been redeemed. So, if you thought that your life was without redemption, THINK AGAIN!

Free from SHAME

I constantly meet women who are rooted in shame. I know because I was rooted in shame. I guess it really takes one to know one. I know how it feels, looks, responds and talks. If you are rooted in shame, it does not take much to trigger the emotion. Failure caused me to be ashamed. For instance, my plan was to keep my virginity until marriage. That was a personal conviction of mine. But, I tried so hard to produce a right behavior without first understanding my position in Christ but only entered a cycle of wrong behavior. I felt horrible. It was the lowest of low for me. More than the mistake, the view that I drew from it about myself triggered more wrong behavior.

I could not even look in the mirror without hating what I saw. I know what it feels like to be a Christian, make a mistake, especially a sexual one, and then feel like a fraud. After this, you're harassed with thoughts like, "You're not as holy as you thought you were," or "God will never forgive you for that." I know all about it. Wrong decisions produce a downward spiral of toxic reactions, such as more wrong decisions, thinking, and perspectives.

FORGIVEN

There is so much to be said about forgiveness or the lack thereof. "Forgiveness is a spiritual practice that allows a person to look beyond the faults, opinions judgments of self or another with compassion for the purposes of being open to endless possibilities." –Iyanla Vanzant. I actually took Iyanla's forgiveness course when I needed to foster forgiveness for myself and others. I needed some extra help with this. I could not wrap my head around forgiving people who hurt me. So, I hid the anger in my religious belief that said "I am not a good Christian if I am angry." Moving forward requires forgiveness. What helped me tremendously was remembering that I had been forgiven for much. I hurt some people along the way as well. They forgave me. Some of them did. Others, not so much. I needed to return the favor of forgiving others. And it took humility, maturity and openness to change. It also takes a retrospective look at SELF! The truth is that we all need to forgive or have needed to be forgiven for faults at some point in our lives. The one thing that I was forgetting in this vital principle was to forgive myself. I couldn't forgive others until I knew how to forgive myself. It's funny how we always forget to do the thing that should be the most natural, and that is to extend grace to ourselves. These principles not only work on others, they work on SELF. When we get self together, THEN we can change the world.

Free from CONDEMNATION

As I was beginning to understand more about the nature of God's love, I identified condemnation in my life. I realized that God did not want me to operate from a place of thinking that He was holding my sins against me. Rather than condemnation, God wants to make us aware of what's wrong and correct it. We call this conviction. Conviction is a harsh word, thinking from a real world perspective. BREATHE! God's conviction is like the sensor on a car that warns when the threat of hitting another car is present. So, it's not to be confused with being convicted in a courtroom. Those signals have saved my life because they have come as a warning when I was about to do something before thinking twice.

Conviction has a great purpose that I have come to appreciate. But of course, the enemy perverts every gift that God provides. I expect those warning signals. They are necessary because sometimes, we are genuinely unaware of potential sin, while other times, we are. Let's be honest. Conviction is vital in the life of a REAL woman.

John 3:17 is one of the most compassionate scriptures that I've read in the moments of condemnation. It says,

" For God did not send the Son into the world in order to judge (to reject, to condemn, to pass sentence on) the world, but that the world might find salvation and be made safe and sound through Him."

I AM ESTEEMED BY GOD

Do you want to know the number one reason you do not esteem yourself? Here it is—you don't know how much your Creator esteems you. It's true! You don't believe that what's on the inside of you has the ability to change you, cities, regions, nations and the world. You don't think that you are worth being honored, respected, valued and prospered. You believe that God created you, but subconsciously think that maybe He left something out. The scarcity mindset continues to echo, "I'm missing something." This attitude will never yield a fulfilling life. And more than likely, you will never understand your value.

One of the major identity crises of our times is that we are suffering from another person's estimation of who we are. With such dependent personalities, our self-esteem is left extremely poor. But, I have discovered from my own experiences with lack of self-discovery that self-esteem is essential for our health and survival. Dr. Nathaniel Branden says, "How we feel about ourselves literally affects EVERY aspect of our experience, from the way we function at work, in love, in sex, to the way we operate as parents to how high in life we are likely to rise." Your esteem is your ability to be respectful of the identity that you have been given.

Knowing your Creator means you know that what He gives is guaranteed. Your identity is the image of God; this alone gives you value. The estimated value that you have given yourself will determine how you live your life. Self-esteem or the lack thereof is not based on external factors, but is hinged on the clarity that you have gained about yourself. Some of us look in the mirror and think or verbalize the worst about ourselves. For example, I used to look in the mirror and say, "I hate the way I look being this skinny." Self-esteem is not based on physical attributes, but when there is no acceptance of the physical attribute, lack of love for one's overall self will be present. I disrespected my physical self to the point of disliking who I was. But after I learned my value, I now say that I have a nice, slim frame, and I want to see about adding a few pounds to fill out my clothes a little bit more. Which type of self-talk do you think had a negative effect on my self-esteem? Only the obvious, I HATE THE WAY I LOOK BEING THIS SKINNY. Just that thought clobbered my self-esteem. This may seem so obvious, but we still do it. This causes us to spiral into the scarce mentality, resulting in dishonorable behavior. Neither one changes the image in the mirror. Your thoughts change the way you see yourself, which is the basis of having a healthy estimation of yourself.

As a woman who has seen major transformation in my own life through identity discovery, I am on assignment to remind every woman of who she really is in Christ. I am not joining the movement of people telling you that you need to change the world. The world changes when we change. Identity-discovery is personal power. Personal power is a weapon that has many forms. You NEED it. You don't get personal power externally. Personal power is the power we exude when we showcase our ability to forgive, not compare, love, live by boundaries and personal convictions and esteem ourselves. Of those forms, self-esteem is the main force that drives personal power. What is stopping you from being completely confident in who you are? Although each woman has a different experience, without fail, deficient self-esteem can be traced back to one of these three reasons:

1. LACK OF DISCOVERY

When something or someone is held in high esteem, that thing or person has value, but there is a step before that. Because there is NO way to esteem something without first identifying the value. Equally, you can't value something that you don't first know. The idea is that self-esteem comes from self-discovery. Can you describe who you are without tearing yourself down? Do you know your purpose? Your answers are critical to your self-esteem.

2. TOXIC SELF-TALK

"I am fat."
"I don't have anything to offer."
"I am slow."
" I will never be able to make good money."
"I am dumb."
"I will never get it."
"I am too old."
"I am ugly."
"I am skinny."
"I don't know enough."
"I am stupid."
"I can't win for losing."
"I don't have good luck."

Every one of us can identify traits about ourselves that we would like to change or that we don't like as much as the others. Some of us would like to go back in time and erase our pasts, and that's OKAY, but incriminating yourself is not. I get it. I know you think that being the first to highlight your frailties or using the same universally demeaning words to describe the frailty will make you feel better about it, but it doesn't. It actually plummets your self-esteem. Judgmental words or any other negatively descriptive words are the nemesis to a healthy self-esteem. Who gave you permission to use such words against yourself anyway? Just because there is something that you would like to change, does not mean that you get demean yourself. Put some RESPECT on it.

3. LACK OF SELF-ACCEPTANCE

Feeling accepted is one of our basic needs as humans. We all want to belong. However, a common misconception is that acceptance comes from external mediums. The way to meet this need starts with self-acceptance. The first person who needs to accept you is YOU. Self-acceptance breeds healthy self-esteem. The acceptance for yourself is initiated by God's acceptance for you. He provides a special place in His family for you to belong, and you fit perfectly there. So, if He accepts you, take your cue from Him, but don't just look to accept the strengths without the weaknesses. It's ALL or NOTHING!! Self-acceptance does not mean that faults and frailties don't exist. It simply means that there is a healthy realization that the present may not be the best you. In fact, self-acceptance is the prerequisite for change. For example, if you have said that you are not happy with your current weight, before you decide to even lose a pound, you have to first fall in love with and accept the present you. Respect where you are. Respect for where you are will push you into being the best you.

How to Develop a Healthy Self-Esteem

1. Understand what your creation process means for you. I think about the natural process of a pearl because it's intrinsic to the pearl's value. I'm talking about a real pearl. There is nothing that can imitate the phenomenon of a pearl's creation. The same is true for you. Remember that you were fearfully and wonderfully made in the image of God. You are an extension of Him. This alone makes you valuable.
2. Know who you belong to. The fact that you belong to God gives you value. You would be common if you did not belong to God. Here is a thought. Items owned by celebrities gain value because of who the celebrity is. Without the celebrity, the picture would just be a picture and the shoes would just be shoes. The same is true for you. You are the workmanship of God. He owns you. You are HIS—PERIOD! This ownership multiplies your value to no end.
3. Know your self-worth. No amount of money can be given to exceed the cost that Jesus paid for you. His death paid for your life. To date, He is the biggest ransom known to humanity. No one can

pay you what you are worth. Stop discounting yourself. Knowing your self-worth increases your net-worth.
4. Eliminate all judgmental self-talk. Eliminate words like ugly, dumb, stupid, fat, buckteeth, bald-headed, slow, bad hair, bitch, big lip, big head, skinny, can't, and all other demeaning words. You might have been using these words against yourself for your whole life. Now you have to find positive and encouraging words to use as descriptions for who you are. Create a new normal for talking about yourself. Here are some examples of how you can replace judgmental statements with compassionate self-descriptions.
Judgment: I don't have anything to offer.
Compassion: I am more than enough and I improve daily.

Judgment: Who am I to be successful?
Compassion: I deserve and will live the life of my dreams on my terms. My success brings God pleasure.

Woman of God, you are one of the most complex organisms that God created. The fact that you have been made in the image of God shows His estimation of you. He did His best work when He made you. This was an intentional process, not an accidental one. Psalms 139 lets you know that God made you fearfully and wonderfully. You can't and will not be duplicated. After creating you, He looked at you and gave Himself a compliment, saying, "It's good." You are esteemed, honored, blessed, prospered, anointed and called by God. No one can take this from you.

5. Accept yourself. *See below.*

I AM ACCEPTED BY GOD

Self-acceptance is essential for psychological well-being, but fostering acceptance for ourselves can be extremely difficult. For some of us, our childhood conditioned the belief that acceptance follows good work, resulting in a negative view of ourselves due to less than desirable behavior. So, self-acceptance became based on conditions. A high level of love is needed to foster acceptance for yourself because you will have to come to terms with the past as well as your perceived flaws. Some of them, only you know about.

Self-acceptance is not dismissive of the need to mature and develop. If not careful, the desire for acceptance can become a desperate cry for attention. This causes us to be deceived into believing that the only way that we can be loved is by working for it. Consequently, people start allowing others to take advantage of them, their self-esteem plummets, they become addicted to approval and develop many other characteristics that are not becoming of their REAL identities. The world is waiting for you to accept who you really are as God already has.

You are reading this book because you are unstoppable, bold, resilient, complete, set aside for God's use, chosen, and developing, yet, not without flaws and shortcomings. You know that there is still some unrealized potential and untapped aptitude that must be exposed. God made you so wonderfully that people will not be able to ignore you or forget you. ACCEPT IT!

I AM LOVE

If there is a group of people who God created with super powers, it's women. YES! YOU have superpowers! SEVERAL! At least, I believe you do. What can I say?! You are quite an amazing woman. You can accomplish anything. It took a woman to shift humanity. Women bring the best and the worst out of men. Women will take care of ANYONE; in most cases, more than one person at a time. Women build empires and a woman led tens of thousands of slaves to freedom. Women have sent rockets to the moon, won Pulitzer prizes, flown or swam across the Atlantic Ocean, served in the Supreme Court, won Oscars and the list goes on and on. We are also breaking through to dominate in industries that our male counterparts have formerly dominated. Women continue to make achievements in science, politics, sports, entrepreneurship, corporate America, literature and art, to name a few. Despite our list of incredible achievements, we have been overlooked historically. However, for some reason, God has preserved the resurgence and uprising of women to now. You are included in the uprising. The world is waiting for you to rise up and take your position.

You have an uncanny knack to nurture other people with love. Love is your superpower. However, we sometimes overestimate this particular superpower. I'd like to qualify the statement. We think that when God said love our neighbors that it meant to love our neighbors more than we love ourselves. Some may feel the need to love others first. Without fail, we actually gave this a try. Sometimes, for so long and without knowing we are doing it wrong until we felt burnt out, used or taken advantage of. We extend love to everyone else first, thinking that we will be able to effectively care for ourselves with leftover energy, compassion and desire. Usually the effort is an epic fail. In general, it looks good to put others first publically until private time exposes a lack self-love. We then justify our lack of self-love by saying, "The Bible says love your neighbor." Indeed, it does. It actually says love your neighbor *as* you love yourself. Chronologically, we see that it says love your neighbor before we see "as yourself," but the execution of this instruction is done in the reverse order. The word "as" gives it away. In this text, "as" means "with the same measure or in the same way." This is because you can only love others to the degree that you love yourself. Love your neighbor the same way you love yourself, NOT before you love yourself and definitely not more than you love yourself. I know they told you not to be selfish and to think about others before you think about yourself. I KNOW! But after years of living by this, I realized that some of the principles that I was loyal to should be illegal. This is one of them! Could it be that your close attention to the well-being of others has been the detriment of your own personal power? Personal power includes your self-esteem, resilience, self confidence, boundaries, ability to be self-directed and self- respect? Think about it! Daily, I realize that if I don't take care of myself first, I will not be able to care properly for anyone else.

Here is a real world situation. For example, when you are getting ready to take a flight, the flight safety video is shown. One of the key instructions states, "If the cabin pressure changes, the panel above you will open, releasing oxygen masks. Reach up and pull the mask towards you, place the mask over your nose and mouth and adjust the mask if necessary. Breathe normally and know that oxygen is flowing, even if the bag does not inflate. **BE SURE TO ADJUST YOUR OWN MASK BEFORE ADJUSTING OTHERS.**" This part of the instruction is key to survival if you think about it. How much help can you be to someone if you can't breathe? Love works the same way! It turns out that from a safety instruction, we can extract a real-life principle.

"How you love people is totally determined by how well you get along with and love yourself."~Dr. Myles Munroe

One of the most important missions in life is to master the art of self-love, but lately, I have been hearing people say that love is self-less. I beg to differ. Love is not self-less. The secret to living a life of service and dedication to others is self-love. No one can benefit from trying to fit into a paradigm that has no biblical, scientific or logical backings. This is not to stop one from being of service to others, even while in a place of need. After a while, pouring without being refilled can be more painful than helpful. My ability to love those who curse me, threaten my life, and TRY ME is from a place of self-love. We can offer so much more to people when we learn how to love properly. Self-love is the very profound prerequisite for being able to turn the other cheek. Love becomes easily dispersed when self-love is considered first. Your ability to be selfish will determine the quality of relationships you have personally, socially and professionally.

Similar to being perfect, being selfish has gotten a bad rap because we have reduced the meaning to its lowest term. We determine that it ONLY means being self-absorbed or keeping knowledge, material items and the limelight to ourselves. That's actually the downside of being selfish. Ponder these questions: How can you teach people how to overcome comparison without first beating it? How can you destroy poverty if you live in it? How can you buy groceries for a single mother if you don't have money? We have to take the stigma off of the word "selfish", and once we do this, we can move in it from a healthy perspective.

"The most important person you need to love is yourself."~ Dr. Myles Munroe

I think you need to say this with me. **I LOVE MYSELF BECAUSE I AM LOVE!**

You are powerful, but not in your own strength. Let that superpower that you have work for you, not stress you out and kill you. The only way to do this is by accepting God's love and allowing Him to show you how to love properly. Only God provides the ability to love yourself. He commands us to love Him, love self and love others. Yes, in that order. We learn in Mark 12: 30-31, which says, "Love the Lord your God with all your heart, soul and mind and with all your strength." Our love for God has to become a priority. From this place, He will provide wisdom on how to use your superpower to intimately love Him, yourself and extend love to the world. Mark 12 is telling us to pursue that type of intimate relationship with God if we want to be exposed to love on this level. That's when you will begin to love the way He loves. The more you love Him, the more you will start to love yourself. This qualifies you to love others correctly.

"When loving others is done incorrectly, the results are being played like a game, not considering your own worth, overcompensating for your time and having thoughts about hurting yourself. That's dangerous and that's not love." ~Crystal Craddieth

To receive God's love for you today, it's important to understand that God's love predates your existence, so you can't do anything good enough to deserve it or anything so bad that you become undeserving of it. God made you as an extension of Himself. He has to love you! You are literally a part of Him. Make the conscious decision to love yourself TODAY.

Remember this about God's love:
1. God's love is unconditional, unmerited and undeserved. God's love can't be explained or measured because it's not based on a condition.
2. God's love is everlasting and eternal. He loves you in the same way that He loves His Son, Jesus.

Will you allow the REAL you to stand up? Of course, you will. Nothing can delay her but you. You have the courage to believe the best about yourself. The REAL you is depending on it. Get bold and ask God to help you manifest your REAL identity! After this, expect Him to make good on His promise. Your request will not intimidate Him.

When I asked God, "Who am I?" He answered me in a tangible way. I literally felt His presence consume me. He said, "You're REAL. You are Righteous, Esteemed, Accepted and Loved." The same is true for you. And nothing can change it. This is your identity and the Holy Spirit has sealed it. There is no-thing, no person and no devil that can break through whatever is sealed by the Holy Spirit. There is nothing wrong with needing a push, counseling or a mentor. We all need help getting through some of the worst times in our lives. We were born with this great power, but we have to discover it and learn how to use it to our benefit.

At the end of each day, I often reflect on the day and ask myself if I have truly exemplified what it means to know who I am and if every decision reflected that knowledge. The answer is not always a resounding yes. On some nights, I can say yes, and those nights outweigh the ones that I answer no. I have bad days, just like everyone else. I guarantee you that you will look at yourself and think about REAL in a new light. It's time to "Get REAL" because the way to win in life is to live a REAL life.

CHAPTER 11

Five Breathing Principles for a Better Quality of Life

"The best way to maintain concentration, according to Mr. Galloway is to focus on your breathing. When your intellect accompanies your breathing rhythm in and out, it's kept occupied, and you tend to experience relaxation and inner peace."
~Anders Olsson

There are five breathing principles that promote optimal living. Each will help you become more aware of your personal style and improve your overall quality of life.

Usually, when I have a cold, I breathe through my mouth and my nose is packed with tissue. Isn't that what you do? How else can you breathe if your nose is not working? Packing my nose with tissue is my last resort, and even though this is improper, it beats not breathing at all. The problem is, having a packed nose interrupts the cadence of proper breathing and leaves no room for nasal breathing. For the amount air you need to breathe properly, while in a relaxed state, your nose is ideal. Nasal breathing can help regulate the amount of air coming and leaving because of its narrow passageway, since your body was created to automatically know how much air it requires. When we don't understand the concept of conscious breathing, there is no way to fully optimize the power of the breath. Therefore, the opportunity for the body to function properly is compromised. Similar to our psychological design, we are physically wired for a great way of being. However, when we don't practice intentional living, we work against the success that we were designed for.

God's brilliance is shown in every part of our design. He was indeed intentional about your entire makeup. You thought that the hairs in your nose were just annoying little pricks serving no purpose other than to make you look bad. Nope! God is more creative than that. Your body feeds on clean air. So, the hairs in your nose have the function of filtering out dirt and pollutants that get into the nose from the environment. This is similar to the function of a water filter on the faucet of a sink. It filters out bacteria found in water. Your mouth does not do that. It does not filter the bad air from the clean air. That's why breathing out of your mouth should be only be done as the last resort. Not to mention the fact that breathing from your mouth changes the natural position of our tongue against our teeth, which increases the risk of you having warped facial features and crooked teeth, according to Anders Olsson. When we embark on the journey of improving our spiritual and psychological breathing habits by becoming intentional, we will begin to really see God's plan materialize in our lives. Proper breathing makes the difference in living and designing your ideal life. No one living a great life is doing it on accident.

"We all have two choices: We can make a living or we can design a life." ~ Jim Rohn

After having struggled for so long with my identity, it took a mental shift for me to see how to reset my life. I had to wash my brain from all of the residue of my past, whether it came from my own toxic behaviors and transgressions or adverse experiences that I faced. When certain elements have removed from your life, the new task becomes training yourself to live without that element. You will have to create a new normal with the new space. The process already started when you began eliminating certain irrational beliefs and thinking patterns. Your brain is now recording positive dialog and creating new neural pathways for a change. Let the new positive dialog serve as the new inspiration for beliefs and thoughts.

I started with extending forgiveness to myself. By doing so, I opened my heart to accept another chance. I developed a longing for authenticity. I became more mindful of my breathing, thinking and living, which really can all be one. The attitude of what I can gain materialistically was fading. I was learning that what I can add and what's on the inside is indeed more valuable. The changes that were taking place and that are still taking place in my life are exciting. The more success I experience, the more aggressive I become. When I finally quit the comparison race, I was able to focus on my mission and what I need to do in order to achieve optimal breathing. The boldness to stand up for myself flourished when I embraced the extra courage to say no, love myself and live by boundaries. I was designing a new lifestyle by going after my dreams, rather than someone else's expectations. For once, I began to get a glimpse at destiny. I felt my breath regulating and the struggle to breathe was finally subsiding. I did not want this feeling of growth to go away. I realized that all of my previous challenges came to introduce me to this new woman that I am becoming. My daily thought is, "From here, my life only gets better and it's totally up to me." Experiencing growth caused me to furnish my destiny with the new vitality and vigor that it takes to expand my life into what I call the REAL life.

In order to guarantee that you take control of your destiny, I want to share with you five principles that I have implemented into my life. They have literally taken my life and others' to the next level. They help you to revive your life, create a powerful version of yourself and stay the course when life gets tough.

If you would like to deepen your fundamental knowledge of yourself and build your faith to see your future as bright, get rid of all of the old programming that goes against the REAL you. The opportunity is yet before you. Since the brain is ever-changing and creating, the life you crave is ever before you and in your reach. It doesn't matter where you are in your life. You can start over. Commitment to these principles is key.

They are…

SELF-DISCOVERY

"Resolve to know thyself and know that he who knows loses his misery" ~Matthew Arnold

Self-discovery defines your life. Increasing the awareness of our identities, we repel the cunning advances of manipulative people, we make connections and discoveries about our strengths, and we discover our innate abilities and gifting. You can refer back to Chapter 2 for the benefits of self-discovery. The list of I AM statements are extremely important as well. I will emphasize a few here. If you are struggling with making solid decisions, perhaps you are not clear about YOU! The first most important accomplishment for a successful life is self-discovery. There is nothing to gain from mastering a career or a subject and not knowing who you are. Discovering yourself will help you start and maintain a great relationship with yourself. This is not to be confused with discovering what others think about you. You will actually be able to think for yourself, thus, making your needs a priority. You can't give to anyone what you are lacking in your own life. Trying to do so slows the supply of oxygen to your brain, thus, causing poor brain function.

Self-discovery means, finding purpose, assignments and gifting while allowing the discovery to create the life that you defined as your "best life". It's no doubt that lack of self-discovery causes purpose to be stifled, which creates a risk for depression and anxiety. Until identity is discovered, you will be a victim of the world's labels and your own misconceptions, never being able to provide any real value to the community and this generation.

Belief precedes confidence. Confidence is assurance that arises from the appreciation or belief in one's own ability. I also find that preparation boosts my confidence. Self-discovery is the preparation for life. Therefore, confidence is an attribute that we all need in our pursuit of this great life. With confidence, you will be able to pursue your goals, rather than executing someone else's plan for you. It's easy to fall into the trap because people say, "I'm expecting this/that from you." This causes pressure because you start to feel like if you don't meet their expectations, you are not doing something right. Faking then becomes the resolve.

Self-discovery eliminates that pressure to conform and compare. Our ability to function at our best, as multidimensional creatures, hinges on self-knowledge. Knowing who you are gives you a boldness that can only increase. When your mind and brain records this boldness, it gives you the ability to function highly in a world that is declining.

We are unable to define ourselves as God's children without full awareness of the gift, assignment and purpose that we have for belonging to Him. Self-discovery is seeing yourself through God's lens and using what you have to aid in your success. One of the physical parts of our bodies that we have to aid in our breakthrough of self-discovery is our brains. The brain is literally a computer. It is pertinent that we understand the power of our brains and breath as individual components that work together to create a desired outcome. Contrary to what we were taught, our brains did not stop developing when our bodies stopped. Fairly recent discoveries from decades of research show that the brain does not stop changing, learning and developing. It was created to work for the span of your life. With rigorous consistent effort, you can make strides in the direction of your choice.

In order to find out how to use self-discovery to rewire your brain and reroute your life for greatness, we have to determine our gifts, who we are, assignments and purpose (GWAP). Please dig deeply to find your answers. You may also refer back to previous chapters for guidance.

Gift

To determine gifting, you must ask yourself, "What God-given abilities do I have that will help me solve a problem?" Gifts are unable to be taught. They can only be developed or stirred up as the Bible would have it. Can you teach, sing or counsel others by innate ability? The gift that you have will help you to perform your purpose and your assignment.

Who are You?

This is a very specific description of who you are, with no titles or any extra fluff that we use to bring definition to ourselves. It must be void of outside influence, because jobs can be taken and money can be spent, but no one can stop you from being who you are. Remember, the REAL you is who you are at your soul, not who you had to become to cope with toxic emotions and situations. Who you become spiritually after
accepting Christ does not change. Nothing you can do will change that position. However, who you are naturally can change. That means, if you have become programmed by trauma, you can change and experience post-traumatic growth. The same brain that helped you think of yourself as a failure or a mistake is the brain that can create optimism and see yourself as a success.

Describe your value system. What are the top five things you value in order from the greatest to the least? Time, energy and effort will be spent on what is valued the most.
What do you want? This is a question that works hand-in-hand with value systems. I noticed that religion and experiences can sometimes make us believe that what we want does not matter. NOT TRUE!! Once you are in sync with God's will for your life, He gives you the desires of your heart. That is, if your desires are really from Him. Are you clear on what that is? I know you want to live your best life, but what does that look like? This can't be based on pursuing what looks better. I am asking about your genuine personal desires. What are you willing to contribute to life to get what you want? What are you hungry for? Where would you like your life to take you?

What is the internal or external chatter that is keeping you from going after what you want? Religious beliefs, past experiences, discouragement, and doubt will prohibit you from believing that your wants matter. Other elements may tell you that you are not going to get your wants fulfilled. Both are lies. Your wants matter and you can have what you want. Do you want to be an entrepreneur or are you okay with living the W-2 lifestyle? Do you want to be single or married? Either is great, but are you clear about which one you want? Identifying the chatter that opposes what you want will help you break cycles of getting results that you don't want.

Describe your ideal emotional and mental state. Self-discovery warrants good mental health. A person who is committed to self-discovery understands that change and growth happens on a continuous basis. It never stops. As self-discovery continues, it is an automatic way to protect your heart, realize you power and take control over your life. This is not to say that your mental health will not be challenged with problems. More importantly, it will activate the resilient nature that you are made of. Life will not be able to throw a perplexity that you can't recover from.

- What is your plan to overcome hardships and mental hurdles?
- Can you tolerate strong negative emotions and do something productive with them?
- Do you embrace change?
- Can you say no without feeling guilty?
- Do you let people limit your joy?
- Can you forgive without an apology?

A new blog is released weekly on the subject of developing mental and emotional toughness. Some are universal, but your plan of developing mental toughness has to be unique to you. Allow your unique experiences to aid in your plan for developing mental toughness. I know for sure, your plan must not be developed based on your primitive desire for ease.

What are your strengths and weaknesses? Don't ignore part two of this question. You will need to know where you are weak. Many people just highlight their strengths, not taking into account that weaknesses have their place. Most employers ask the question, "What are your weaknesses?" This is not a trick question, but rather a question designed to assess whether or not you are self-aware. You have to know where there are opportunities for improvement. If you don't, you might not get the job. They are looking for those who have an in-depth knowledge of who they are, the value they can offer and where there is room for improvement. Your weaknesses actually help you in creating winning situations for achieving your goals.

Assignment

Your assignment is the specific project or task you will perform as an extension of your purpose. For instance, my purpose is to revive the lives of people of faith by calling them into who they are. Specific assignments that help me to perform this purpose are speaking to survivors of commercial sexual exploitation, survivors of domestic violence abuse and ex-offenders in transition on the subject of setting boundaries. You will have to know what you will and will not tolerate. I will not tolerate my sisters being oppressed by the trauma of their pasts.

Purpose

What is your purpose? Years ago, people asked me, "What can you do everyday for free?" This question has potential, but it is not fully ripened. No one, especially in my generation, really wants to think about doing anything that would not create revenue, so it does not yield an accurate or authentic response. I dislike this question because it's based on the human desire of something for nothing. We have the mandate to reach every corner of the Earth. Money will aid this goal. This is not to say that you shouldn't give your time to charitable causes.

A better question to discover purpose is…

How can my gifts be used to help me create an impact and solve problems in the area that I am most passionate about? Will I be committed to this over the long haul?
Use this formula.

GIFT + IMPACT + PASSION + COMMITMENT = PURPOSE

Each element of the equation has to be represented. Passion without gift will fail, and vice versa.

Another question to think about is this…
What product or service can I create that would transform someone's life if they invested in it?

Understanding who you are as an individual and as a woman is very important. As a woman, you have a distinct gift that you bring to this Earth, and in order to deliver it, you must activate honor to yourself. You will have to immerse yourself in God's idea of you by cultivating a lifestyle of devotion to Him. When you are ready to be presented to the world, God will make sure your cup is full enough to serve others. He will eliminate the need to worry about missing something. You will have lifetime access to His supply. So, don't worry yourself with thinking that someone can take your place. You have an assignment that makes you valuable to your generation, your family, this world and generations to come. Get clear about what that is. There is a reason you are the way you are. There is a reason you lived with depression for half of your life. There is a reason your dad left. Insert your particular situation. Whatever it is, there is a reason beyond yourself that it happened. When you ask yourself these questions, be sure to sit and listen for an organic answer. The answers will provide clarity and direction for your life.

Self-discovery will require a lot of you, but don't get overwhelmed. You were created to discover one of the greatest people to ever live. That's YOU. Embrace the journey. Just because God put your purpose before you does not mean that there will be no struggle or additional costs. God has already written who you are and etched your identity in stone. You will spend the rest of your life developing into that person. Knowing who she is will start the journey.

CREATE A VISION FOR YOUR LIFE

Every step forward starts with vision.

Vision brings clarity to who you are. Interestingly, it's hard to stay motivated if you're not clear on what you want. After suffering through disappointments, failures and misfortunes, every step forward that you take will start with vision. Vision is the ability to see beyond current and past capabilities, stress and traumas. Vision is really the only way to push through a failure. Think about all of the times you failed at something. You pushed through because there was a glimpse of what could happen if you moved forward. Vision is your ability to see the green pastures ahead from where you are.

Every year, we commemorate Dr. Martin Luther King, Jr. for his vision. His speech entitled "I Have a Dream" was simply his vision for a better America. In the face of riots, segregation and hate crimes, he was able to see the same country that was experiencing hatred, experiencing love, peace and unity. While we still see signs of hatred flaring up, we are living in MLK's vision. It's because of his vision that segregation ended and Blacks and Whites came together. His vision will never be erased from history.

On a personal note, vision helps me to see myself in my dream home from a room in my mother's house. It helps me to see myself happily married, even though I completely bombed what would have been great relationships. It helps me to see myself speaking in arenas and auditoriums full of women around the world when I have not even spoken to a crowd of over 300 people yet. Vision is powerful and takes intentional focus and discernment to develop. Without vision, you will subject yourself to remaining somewhere that you were never meant to stay.

While we usually start small on our paths to greatness, we are not subjected to thinking small. You may have to start with a small budget, a small team, or a small space. Regardless of the physical limits, your vision should expand beyond the limit. Seeing yourself in a bigger place in your mind will cause those physical limitations to be removed. Since, you have a peculiar assignment, your vision will lead the way because technically, trailblazers and first movers don't have a blueprint to follow.

When you close your eyes and dream about your life, what do you see? What do you want to see? I know that's an oxymoron. You can't see if you close your eyes. But when you close your eyes, you can see with a better set of eyes. This does not require natural sight. It requires a convergence of your faith with God's plan and an imagination.

Vision helps you in your day-to-day decision-making process. You can easily make decisions that affect your well-being for the better. Your decisions depend on your vision, so it follows that if you can't see, then you can't decide. Vision does not mean that you will not hit rough spots or that you will do everything right. But you will never lose sight of where you are headed and you will not wallow in your mistakes.

Most people want to live their best lives. You're likely one of them. How do I know? I know because we are wired to live in success. You desire what you are made of. Also, you say it in more ways than one. And the truth is you can AND YOU WILL, but not without knowing what your best life looks like. There is no way to reach your best self without defining who she is and what she wants. Women who've made history had a vision of their lifetimes of achievements.

Where there is no vision, the people expire and become obsolete. (Proverbs 29:18). Excitement and motivation are products of vision and should reflect the greatness of your purpose. Your vision for your future includes every dimension of your life.

That's why you have to write it, not just on the tablets of your heart, but on paper or somewhere that you can refer to it. It's too large to remember. If you can remember it, it's not BIG enough.

Benefits of Vision

Vision chooses your battles. This is based on the idiom that we all hear often. At some point in our lives, most of us have been given the advice to choose our battles wisely. As often as we hear this great advice, we don't think about the cost to forgo one battle to engage in another. When vision is clear, conflict can always be avoided, but it takes practice. I've avoided battles by intentionally taking a conversation that was meant to be an insult and redirecting it to less offensive dialogue. To do this, I could not wear my feelings on my shoulders. I also ask myself if choosing to take the combative route would help me achieve a goal or take me further away from it. Vision does not mean that insults won't sting, but you will become less combative because your time and effort will be spent on what's most important.

Vision increases the value of time. I wish that I would not have fallen into the, "you don't have to make a decision right now" mindset because it provides people with an excuse to be indecisive and waste time doing nothing. This mentality is antithetical to vision. Let me just clarify what I mean. When I was growing up, older people habitually told us younger people, "You are young. You've got time. You don't have to make a decision right now. You don't have to know what you want this soon." They had great intentions. However, without the proper motivation from parents, teachers and spiritual leaders to help us excel, we almost subconsciously choose a slower path. This mindset destroys vision and that's why many people grow up and become serial procrastinators, thinking they have time. This is because we give permission to lack vision. I was one of those people. So, guess what destroys procrastination? You guessed it—vision.

Vision dictates whether or not you allocate your money within a budgetary constraint. Printing a bank statement can really reveal a person's heart and whether or not they have vision based on their day-to-day spending. People who budget their earnings have great financial vision. Some think that a budget is limiting, but it's a vision for the purpose of financial control. Vision will take us further than a bag and shoes or any other type of material possession. Vision will lead us to investing in properties and financial products that gain interest over time.

Vision dictates focus. You may not be able to live a spontaneous life, depending on your goals. Don't allow anyone to hold that against you. Recently, I turned down an invitation to go to the Hawks' game. Being able to do it made me smile. Before I had a vision for my life, I would have never EVER been able to turn down such an invitation. Not to mention floor scats, thc networking and the fun! I needed to focus on something very important to my business. While I love the person who invited me and she apparently knows that I love the Hawks, I could not go. My business took precedence. While I thought I was building my business, there are often times when I felt like my business is building me. I had to keep telling myself that there would be a plethora of opportunities for me to attend a Hawks' game. And my friend totally understood. I love friends that understand my life and don't cause me any grief when I have to decline an invitation.

Time is worth money and nowadays, I don't offer myself to anything that is not in alignment with my vision, even if it is something that is great. Don't confuse this with thinking that I don't help others. My life is dedicated to service. Nowadays, if the assignment does not support my purpose, I won't do it. So, no longer do I volunteer myself for odd jobs. I don't have time to teach a class about how to groom a dog. I'm not going to a conference about how to fly a drone. Time does not come back and should be used wisely. When I lacked vision, it took me longer to finish something (remember, it took me ten years to earn one degree). Without vision, I could not see the time that I was wasting.

One thing about life is that it comes to test your vision without permission. Based on the powerful life that you are created for, you need an authentic vision so that you won't be made into an impostor by life's tests. If you decide to do something just because, it will show in the quality of work you produce, and it won't carry authentically. That's why we should be clear on what we want. Vision is the clarity that we need.

Now, let's do the work. Your written vision details what you want in every area of your life. As you begin writing your vision, make sure you are in a quiet place so that you can hear from within. Your life is yearning to be led by the vision that is already known in the depths of your heart. In order to get answers, strategic questions must be answered. Some questions are fun and just to make you think creatively. For others, you will need to dig deeply for the answers that you need. Your best life is inside of you and it awaits your discovery of it. Some of the questions that help you create your vision were asked in the first breathing principle. Vision starts there. Feel free to add your own questions.

Here are three areas of vision and the details to accompany the vision. Allow these examples to help you when you start writing your vision.

Personal Vision for Financial Independence and Personal Development

I am birthing an online empire that will be the solution for improving the psychological state of the world, one person at a time. Thousands of women from around the globe will enroll in my courses to enrich their lives. I will always believe in myself and learn from my mistakes. Through commitment to serving others, I will continuously pursue new ideas, gain mastery over self-discovery and become a mental health expert. I will always live by my words and model, with conviction, what I teach. I will master the challenges of life so as to be a light to those who know me. I will use my struggles and my victories to create value for others. My pursuit of excellence will guide my decisions so that poverty will never find its way back to my address. Details: create online courses and products that address the needs of women in my market. Create a marketing plan, save and invest, money, tell my story through speaking, sell the products, spend several hours daily studying my field, always seek knowledge and learn various perspectives.

Personal Vision for Mental and Emotional Health

I will always maintain awareness of how life's challenges are impacting me. I will take bold new challenges with deliberation and heart. If things go awry, I will embrace change. I will control my dealings with toxic people by keeping my heart in check. I will always satisfy the needs of my soul. It's important that all rcsiduc from past trauma is removed, so I will take constant inventory of my heart's condition. I will commit to nourishing my mind with truth, education, and positivity. I will always seek counsel for issues that exceed my ability to cope. I will hold myself and others accountable for their actions and words. I will commit to mental exercises and daily routines that contribute to wellness. My purpose will cause me to stay the course when life gets tough. Details: Practice boundaries, give people permission to dislike me, set myself up for success, understand purpose, reflect on the meaning of events.

Personal Vision Statement for Spiritual Growth

My spiritual life will advance continuously as I commit to working in my calling. I believe that Jesus Christ died for my salvation. Therefore, I will serve Him alone, always respecting, but never intertwining my beliefs and practices with that of another form of religion that is not rooted in Christianity. I will aggressively practice God's presence using spiritual disciplines such as prayer, fasting, studying and meditating as my life depends on it. It's important to me that my life reflects the Word of God, so I will harness the authority that God provides and receive everything that the death, burial and resurrection of Jesus accomplished. I will be the light and the salt of the world by being a great representation of

Jesus Christ everywhere I go. My overall goal is to model the life of Jesus in practicing forgiveness and compassion for others. Details: incorporate faith and beliefs into daily living,

The small details can't be left out. They really make the BIG picture come together. The big picture or vision really streamlines the daily goals and tasks. Everything that you do becomes the vehicle that takes you closer to or further away from your destiny. The following questions will help you unearth the vision for the other areas of your life, such as family, occupational, physical, health and nutrition, educational, social and relational.

1) Are you family-oriented? What is a strength of your family?

2) How many children do you want?

3) What do you know for sure? (I took this question from Oprah.) This is not to be confused with what someone told you.

4) Describe the person you want to spend your life with. What is their love language?

5) What are the qualities of your ideal relationships, both platonic and romantic?

6) Do you work out? If not, will you start and commit to it?

7) What is your diet like? Does it support how you want to look, think and feel?

8) Will you spend a little more money on healthier food choices?

9) What are your spiritual beliefs? How committed are you to your beliefs? Explain.

10) What would help you become more grounded in your beliefs?

11) How diverse is your circle of friends? Do they all think, vote, look, and believe like you?

12) What is it that you should master? Where does your expertise lie?

13) Do you have a personal growth plan? If not, create it based on where you want to see yourself.

14) What books do you need to read? These books support personal and educational goals.

15) Do you need additional education, classes or credentials?

16) How will you invest in yourself?

17) Are you willing to make sacrifices to be the best at what you do?

18) What is your ideal profession? Why?

19) Do you want to be financially independent, meaning that your own resources create your income?

20) Do you have a financial plan?

21) What do you want to make monthly? Annually?

22) Will you own any land?

23) Where do you want to live?

24) Do you have philanthropic interests?

25) How will you challenge yourself mentally, physically, spiritually, and emotionally? What are your needs in each area?

26) What type of car do you want to drive?

27) How many vacations do you take yearly?

28) What excites you? How will you keep life exciting?

29) What frustrates you? Can you use frustrations to propel yourself forward?

30) What do you do to relax or recharge? Do you have a self-care plan?

31) What will you do to develop mental and emotional strength? Establish goals, set yourself up for success, stop negative thinking, set boundaries, etc.

32) Describe your thoughts on a daily basis? Do they have gold or bronze quality?

33) What will you become so good at that people can't ignore you or erase you from history? Why will people remember you?

34) How will you market yourself?

35) What problems can you solve? What answers do you have? What transformation do you provide?

The answers to these questions help your destination become clear and tangible. They make up the pictures on your vision board. You are not limited to my questions. There are hundreds of others. Without you knowing the answers to these questions, a vision board will not provide an elevated perspective. Your life is awaiting your answers to these questions. These questions are the start of your best life, but only if you will answer them and visit them frequently enough to keep them on the forefront of your mind. It's time to see yourself as the great woman that you are. Start writing your vision today!

IMPLEMENT SYSTEMS

"The secret to your success is hidden in your daily routine."
~Dr. Cindy Trimm

Have you ever had a bright idea to create something, the tools to create it, and once the project was started, you could not seem to finish it? That's because, without a system in place to accompany the vision, projects are not executed properly. System is defined as a set of daily routines that have a predictable and specific outcome. And in order to reach your big goals, you need a system. A system brings structure to your vision. It adds feet to your vision and takes the steps toward reaching each milestone that leads to a destination. Systems establish order and structure in your life. The older I get and the more responsibilities that I take on, the clearer it becomes that I am not able to function without systems. They keep me in order and on task. Anyone who knows me, knows how I can get off task easily. Those who consistently knock their goals out of the park are adept at implementing systems. They eliminate distractions.

For a long time, I wondered why I struggled to complete tasks. Realizing that I was ignoring my weaknesses caused a major breakthrough. I needed to develop awareness of my proclivity to get off task in order to confront and change it. My denial was causing cycles of failure and lack of productivity. This is why I highlighted the important role that identifying weaknesses play in setting yourself up for the win. From my discovery, I was able to create a system customized to the way I work, which helps me to stay on task.

With a system, projects can be managed and completed on time. If you are like I was, without it, you will have twenty incomplete projects. I wanted to reach my goals. I deserved to reach them, but without doing the right things, I couldn't. So, when I decided that I wanted to change my eating to match a healthier lifestyle, I created a system. Without it, I would be in Chick-fil-A's drive through on a daily basis.

Every thought-leader of our generation encourages systems, conveying how necessary they were for their success. Being a teacher, a salesperson, freelance writer, nail shop owner, life coach, corporate executive, author and stay-at-home mom all require a system. You won't check off every item on your list in the beginning. The commitment to the system will increase your productivity and cause more consistent success. Nothing can fall through the cracks with a system. Likewise, safety is found in a system.

The most important concept you need to know about systems is that systems should be created to help you optimize your time and efforts for the win. For example, if you are a writer and want to write consistently so that you finish your book, a system is vital. If you are more productive during the earlier part of the morning, you have discovered your ideal time for writing. This will be the time you find your creative flow, and most of your writing should be done then. All things have to be considered. Your strengths and weaknesses go into the creation of systems. This is where even your weakness looks like strengths.

Here is my system for eating a consistent diet.

1. I decide on what I want to eat for the week, breakfast, lunch and dinner.
   Example:
   Breakfast: I want a green smoothie everyday this week.
   Lunch: I will have a spinach salad with blackened salmon.
   Dinner: I will have spaghetti made with zucchini noodles.

2. Create a list by taking inventory of the cabinets to see what I need and what I already have before I take the trip to the grocery store. This is important because buying only what is needed will save you money.
3. Go to the grocery store on Sunday after church.
4. Cook and store. I like to cook and immediately store my food in containers so that I can grab a dish on the way to work, including packing snacks for moments of craving. This saves time and money. It's simple, but it's a system.

You may already be following these tips, but never thought of them as systems. Another system that I am starting to implement is preparing my clothes for the week, from what I will wear to work to my gym clothes. It's literally the same as the meal prepping system. I used to laugh at my friend, Amy Rochon, who had a habit of doing this, but this is a life-saver. Thanks Amy!

1. 1. I decide on what I am wearing, this is includes gym clothes.
2. I take an inventory of my drawers to see if what I have chosen in my head is clean. Sometimes, if I get too relaxed, I will choose what I know I don't have to wash. But, you get the point.
3. If I do need to wash, I'll do it on Saturday mornings. This is the step that will position you for the win. Even if you have made a mental note of what you are wearing, if it's not clean, you can't wear it. Well, you can, but it might stink.
4. Once the clothes are clean, you can hang them for the week or put them in their designated drawers for easy access at any given time.

I normally take 30 minutes to pick out something to wear, so this system lets me sleep a little longer and saves me the headache of picking out clothes in the morning. More complex goals may require more steps. Use your creativity to put systems in place. Systems align with your vision and the day-to-day details that will help your vision become a reality. You must ask yourself, what daily and weekly assignments do I need to complete in order to bring this vision to reality? The answers create your system. Productivity is inevitable when systems are in place. Your life will elevate from good to great with daily practices, especially since success is predictable. You can literally become a high performer. Just implementing these two simple systems can detox your schedule and help you to eliminate some anxiety.

ESTABLISH A BOUNDARY SYSTEM

"What ever you are willing to put up with is exactly what you will have." ~Anon

Establishing boundaries will be a daunting feat until you have the courage to completely remove people from your decision-making process. Likewise, a people-pleasing lifestyle does not support boundaries. Establishing boundaries will also prove to be hard without clarity on what you want.

What are boundaries? Boundaries are limits and borders that protect the energy, time, emotions, spirit, mind, physical space, feelings and anything concerning an individual. Boundaries bring definition to the space between you and an individual or you and an entity. Although challenging, many have proven this boundary system to be possible. I am one of them. But, I learned the hard way that my boundaries are about me. Just like your boundaries are about YOU. What YOU want, what YOU are willing to do, where YOU draw the line, what YOU will put up with. What will YOU tolerate? What type of relationship do YOU want? This allows you to take self-care precautions. I am currently a teacher and one of the things that I repeatedly tell my students is, "The only person you have control of is YOU." You are responsible for your attitude, your actions, and your space. You can only control yourself and no one else.

To become better at honoring who you are, it's imperative to create boundaries aligned with your beliefs, your identity, your values and your VISION. Before now, you probably tried to set boundaries without a clear vision. There is no real way to establish boundaries before becoming clear about who you are, what you want and your purpose. The clarity identifies your limits. Think of it like a property. Every property has a border surrounding it that tells people where the property line (limit) begins and ends. They know where they can go without being considered a trespasser. In order for people to really know where the limits are, property owners put up fences, signs or they'll have some type of indication that tells others where the property line stops and starts. They also insure the property.

Without boundaries, you will find that people trespass onto your property, and they will even litter on your property, as if trespassing is not enough. The trespasser is not to blame in most cases. You have given them power to do what they will because you have not set any clear limitations, and they will not think about how the invasion will affect you. People will deal with you based on the permissions you give them or the power you relinquish. There are some people who are only around because of the power you give them by not having boundaries. Once you begin to establish boundaries, personal motives will be exposed.

From prior chapters, you could likely guess that I did not have clear boundaries. Consequently, I was not confident in using my voice to demand respect. So, there was no way that I could possibly show others how to treat me. I was so afraid that I would lose friends if I practiced this level of self-care. You might not know what your boundaries are, and that's okay. Today, you WILL set boundaries and begin enforcing them immediately. Immediate implementation really helps with remembering how it works. Usually, when you put off starting til the next day, chances are, you won't start. You could forget what you learned by the time you go to bed if you don't take action. This is more of a reason to **START TODAY**!! No, REALLY. When you are done with this chapter, use the steps that you will learn to establish YOUR boundaries. Don't forget to write out your vision first.

By nature, we all crave boundaries in our lives, but like me, you may have settled for comfort because of lies and misconceptions of your past.

You might think…

1. I don't want anyone to think that my boundaries are meant to change them. Actually, boundaries are never about anyone else. They only let people know where you stand as it relates to the situation.
2. Boundaries are too confrontational. Well, I am very confrontational. There is nothing wrong with being confrontational. As long as confrontation is done with tact. Confrontation is a form of communication, which we have discussed. It's a major step in this system. Sometimes, we dodge confrontation because it has gotten a bad reputation. We were never exposed to the proper way of initiating effective confrontation.
3. I might upset or lose a friend. Everyone will not approve of your boundaries. That's expected, BUT these people are not your friends and should not hold any place in your heart. They stand in a different category. You should not want a relationship of any sort with this category of people. A real friend will honor your boundaries.
4. I'm doing it wrong. This was only true before you wrote your vision. It is impossible to set boundaries without knowing what you want, who you are and your purpose. PERIOD. Now, you can use your vision to establish your boundaries in alignment with your vision.

Unfortunately, these misconceptions keep people in cycles of stagnancy and failure so they won't take their true positions in the world. When people know where you stand, they can quickly decide whether to take you or leave you. Give them full permission to leave you. It's completely up to the person to leave or stay. Either way, they are clear as to what they get when they get you. When boundaries are clear, you will stop neglecting your needs to satisfy your true hunger. You will do what it takes to meet your needs, which puts you in the position to take your power back. You are a woman who honors her boundaries and you will be blessed to be around people who honor your boundaries. I dare you to say that with me… "I honor my own boundaries and people around me honor my boundaries as well." Keep saying it until you believe it. You are rewiring your mind to create a new normal.

Every time I did not set boundaries with people, I ended up being hurt at some point in the relationship. I got tired of being hurt, especially when I could control it by making a simple decision. I knew something else needed to happen. I didn't know where to start, but I knew that I did not like the feeling that my life was at the mercy of another imperfect human, one who benefited from my low self-esteem. So, I vowed not to put myself in a situation where I would lose control again. As with forgiveness, following a simple boundary system will allow you to take control of your life. When not dealt with, even the smallest experiences will grow into deeply rooted pain. When I dated, I would often bail out when I thought I was falling in love, especially if I knew that I had not demonstrated any boundaries. Keep in mind that I did not even think I was lovable. I was trying to go with the flow, but I hated the feeling associated with not being in control. This is not to be confused with being in control of the relationship. This is more so about being in control of what I put up with. And with no boundaries, I was never in control because anything could go. I have found that people who have boundaries in place are more likely to respect the boundaries of others.

Why just setting boundaries alone not enough?

After learning that having boundaries played a part in saving my life, I fell in love with the idea of setting boundaries. I make fun out of it. You can do the same. Boundaries must be set for every part of your life, but maybe you've noticed that something is missing from this life skill. That's because it's possible to over-set boundaries and be under-prepared to really practice healthy boundaries as a lifestyle.

Recently, I was teaching a class about how setting boundaries is not enough. Of course, I know this from experience. So, I was bubbling with passion. There are just so many people like myself who love to set boundaries. I can't even begin to tell you how many boundaries I have. I have spiritual boundaries, communication boundaries, relationship boundaries, professional and personal boundaries. I am even creating an online course about how to establish boundaries. I have all these boundaries, but when I solely rely on them, I still come up short. The problem is that we are taught that if we establish boundaries, we will be okay. That is only true to a certain extent. Establishing something is only the beginning. It is important and is necessary to protect yourself when defining the space between you and others. Still, this does not promise sustenance.

Relying too much on establishing boundaries allows the tendency to overlook and ignore the rest of what exists in the boundary system. This is vital for healthy relationships, connecting with yourself first, and disregarding what others think. You will need the full process if you plan on solidifying cohesive, long-term, mutually beneficial relationships, all the while, not losing who you are. You also need this process if you want a life free of mental anguish. If you plan on seeing the results of your boundaries, you need a system that includes: establishing boundaries, communicating boundaries, respecting boundaries and enforcing boundaries.
I want to unpack this just a little bit more.

When I started setting boundaries, I stopped having to set New Year's resolutions yearly. Making New Year's resolutions every year, especially the same ones, just means that there was an inconsistency with respecting my boundaries. Perhaps, I broke a promise or violated a boundary somewhere. I had to realize that the same resolution coming up every year was inconsistency on my end. Think about this. Most New Year's resolutions start something like this: "I'm going to start *back* working out. I'm going to start *back* eating right. I'm going to start *back* saving money. I just want to start taking *better* care of myself." These should be the standard in our lives anyway. This was my invitation to live by a system. This system showed me that I am in control of my own life. I had to do some work to be able to exercise my boundaries and have better relationships and ultimately, have a better life. So, there are things and behaviors that I no longer tolerate from myself and others. PERIOD

Here is the system…

Step 1: Establish your boundaries.

Establishing is simply the decision-making step of the system. You must use your ability to decide. You're drawing the line by saying, "THIS is my limit. I won't do this, I will not take this, I won't take that or I stop right here." Decisiveness is so very important, not just for boundary setting, but in life. Setting boundaries requires loyalty to yourself and recognition of your value. You have to be comfortable with yourself and willing to extend the best care of yourself.

For instance, I have a boundary that I do not participate in yoga or any other spiritual practice that can't be traced to Christianity. NO JUDGEMENT. That's a spiritual boundary for ME. This boundary is in alignment with my personal vision for spiritual growth. I don't believe that my spirit needs to intermingle with other spiritual practices and customs that don't support my Christian beliefs, or more importantly, do not have a Christian origin. I tried yoga before, even as a Christian. I had not done my research concerning its origin. This boundary is based on one of my spiritual visions. Seeing your vision definitely helps in the decision-making step of the process. It does not mean you will not make a mistake or fail, so this first step is just acknowledging that you have limits. THAT IS ALL!

But there are more steps to actually making sure you indeed follow through.

Step 2: Communicate your boundaries.

This is the step that gets overlooked most of the time. Anyone can set boundaries, but having great boundaries without ever communicating them means absolutely nothing! We have the best intentions and we have the desire to be accomplished, but we often forget that we have to put ourselves in the winning position. A lot of times, we will say to ourselves, "This is what I want," but forget all of what goes into being able to actually get what we want. I can't tell you how many times I have set myself up for failure because I simply did not open my mouth and express my limits or disapproval for something, nor did I make a decision about something that affected my well-being. This shows that you love and have compassion for yourself. It may sound selfish, but who cares? If we don't care for ourselves first, how can we continue to take care of others without burning out? This is what you can say to the people who are critical of your self-care.

Everyone won't honor them or always agree, but your boundaries are not for them. You are in control of your self-care when you go public with your limits. Communicating your boundaries empowers you to use your voice and it saves relationships from ruin. People have to know your boundaries in order to adhere to them. You are unable to hold them accountable if you don't give them insight on what your limits are.

Step 3: Respect your boundaries

Adherence to a high personal standards protect against personal problems. Only a serious person with self-love respects their own boundaries. Now, that alone can make the difference between the start of a healthy relationship and one that is a sheer waste of time. This is THE best way to teach people how to treat you. Respecting your own boundaries sends a direct message to your friends because it tells them how serious you are! Or as my former teacher says, it tells them, "You do not play the radio." That's exactly what you want, but there is a caveat. Respecting boundaries is a two-way street. You can't expect for your boundaries to be honored without you first respecting the boundaries of others. It's a dance. Usually, people will respect you if you respect them, and rightfully so. I would question the integrity of anyone who requests that I respect their boundaries, without the urgency to return the favor. There is no way to expect respect where you have not given it.

It's time to act in order to gain control over your life. Talk is cheap. It always has been. Say what you mean and mean what you say and follow through with your actions. If you say no when you mean yes, you create and internal fight and confuse those around you. This delays progress and it creates susceptibility to mental health challenges. The worst person to be at a constant toil with is yourself. When I have said yes and really wanted to say no, I suffered mentally and definitely emotionally. I had to listen to my inner dialogue. It sounded something like, "Why didn't you just say no?! You didn't really want to do it anyway! You can't afford to do that. You knew you had something else to do!" I found myself feeling stuck, trying to turn water into wine in order to make good on a promise. When battling internally, it's hard to be mentally, emotionally and physically present. It is also hard to enjoy family and friends or to achieve anything. You can make yourself sick thinking about what you should have done, so just do it.

The last step, but definitely not the least step of the execution process is…

Step 4: Enforce your boundaries

This is a pivotal step of the process. When someone respects your boundaries, reward them with your trust and your loyal friendship. This person has your best interest at heart and will be someone who will stand the tests of time because the intent of their heart has already been exposed. On the contrary, when boundaries are not respected, consequences should be given. If there are no consequences, we risk being an encourager of destructive behaviors in another. Being an enabler to a taker does more harm than good. You are the boundary enforcement agent. No exceptions should be made for violators. Anyone who expects you to behave outside of your set standards is toxic and should be escorted off of your property.

By being loyal to this system, you will alleviate the mental anguish associated with disrespect and create lasting relationships. You will also remove yourself from toxic situations. Sometimes, it seems easier to remain in toxic relationships because remaining in them requires no change, no confrontation and no work on your behalf. Your comfort might be taxing your health, peace, sanity and your life. This is where clarity on what means the most to you comes into play. *If your peace of mind is not negotiable, then your boundaries should not be negotiable.* Your mental health is the foundation of your total health. Society would love for you to think that life should be lived passively. You have the right to only accept what respects your boundaries. That means, in any situation, feel empowered to make a decision that contributes to your well-being, even if it means leaving, confrontation or saying no.

A lot of times, we think we can make a decision (STEP 1) and then sit back and enjoy life, but there are further actions that are overlooked because we are so focused on the big picture that the small details that make up the big picture are not exposed. So, learn from my mistakes. Now that I have mapped out the system that has helped me to properly set boundaries in my life, I saw it worth sharing with you. You will find that you have better and more beneficial relationships and a drama-free life by using this system.

These Issues Are An Invitation To Create Boundaries

1. You constantly work, feeling responsible for everyone's happiness but your own. You end up feeling used by people for your efforts to remedy their problems.
2. Low self-esteem. A deficient in self-esteem is the source of most pain and suffering in our world. You are not incapable of increasing your self-esteem.
3. Distractions. Your schedule is loaded with tasks that have nothing to do with reaching your personal goals. Rarely will you

say no to invitations, even though invitations come with a choice of YES or NO. If it's not in alignment with your vision and goals, say NO.

4. You continue to accept manipulating and controlling behavior from others. This causes toxic relationships and emotional devastation. Manipulative people will always place your needs on the back burner and never take responsibility for their part in the relationship. Control and manipulation should not have to be endured in the name of love and friendship.

5. You apologize for your wins and play small when you should be putting your uniqueness on display. Women are nurturers and should feel what our sisters feel. We should be moved by their feelings, but not if it means hiding or cheapening our success, competence or happiness. In most cases when your sister has achieved a win, several failures proceeded. You may feel uncomfortable discussing a win with other women. But, it is possible to use your wins to encourage other women to level-up. Your success has the power to bring freedom to others.

6. You don't charge what you are worth. If you know your self-worth, your net-worth increases. If you have taken the time to build influence and create a service or product that solves problems for people, you should do it at the price that makes people take you seriously. Sometimes we think that a lower price attracts more customers. That's not always true. "In some cases your inability to see the value in your products and services can make people think you and your items are a joke or it can attract the wrong customer. Instead of trying to cheapen your prices, continue to add more value"~Suresh May. Your time and expertise are worth money and people pay for results. Charge what you are worth!

7. No clarity of your personal needs and expectations. This is worth saying time and time again. As the master of your soul, you are responsible for making sure your needs are met or you will find yourself disappointed. Disappointment can be avoided by simply being direct and making sure that people know what you want and how you want it.

8. You have a scarcity mindset. You have determined that you are less than, missing something or that you will run out before you

get to who you really are.
9. Your relationships just flow. Flowing in a relationship is actually the response to the stress of not feeling confident that you are worthy to have what you want. Additionally, to go with the flow is to automatically succumb the pull of gravity, which causes matter to go downward and settle. Intention is one of the cornerstones of a relationship, not a flow.
10. Your mental health is suffering. Mental health is vital for your total health. Good mental health comes from being in alignment with the REAL you and making good, solid decisions. You were wired for relationships and boundaries, but might have settled for involvement with no limits. No boundaries cause thoughts to spiral out of control until depression, anxiety and agony control your entire life and define your identity.

The Biblical Side of Boundaries

Let's bring some balance with the biblical context. Did you know the Word of God supports boundaries? IT DOES!! Actually, all of this starts in the Word. God created us to live based on self-care and protection. He does His part in supplying divine protection, but He requires us to set limits and laws in our lives. He tells us several times in the great book that I have been referring to throughout this book, to set and keep boundaries. God commands us by saying, "Guard your heart *above all* else, for it determines the course of your life." (Proverbs 4:23 NLT). God is our father and really wants us to listen carefully to His words, let them penetrate deep into our hearts and use them to live well. Since He is committed to your best interest, He gives this command as a prerequisite for living your best life. When we chose to guard our hearts, we chose the good life.

Your life is delicately attached to your physical and spiritual heart. For this reason, we are commanded to be careful with our hearts and require others to do the same. Starting a business, worrying, deciding to be friends with someone, starting or ending a relationship, being nice or mean, forgiving, killing, or choosing a job, among thousands of other daily decisions, all hinge on the condition of our hearts.

God uses the phrase ABOVE ALL for a specific reason. Above all means before you do anything else and with more effort and attention. The care of your heart takes precedents in your life. And remember, the spirit controls the physical, like the concept of "mind over matter." So, your life will not exceed the health of your heart.

Some of the boundaries I set earlier in life were fear-based and were aimless. So, rather than setting the boundary to keep myself consecrated for God because of my beliefs and my understanding of why He wants me to be pure, my choice to abstain was more based on the fact that I was told that I could not do it. And I was afraid of the results. It's not irony that I have mentioned my sexual sins in more than one chapter because that's where emphasis was placed. All of the examples of sin in sermons are sexual. It gets old. That is RELIGION. When I learned about grace, I set boundaries based on the truth. This requires us to understand God's purpose for our lives. If you do not utilize the gift of boundaries, God says this, "He who has no rule over his own spirit is like a city without walls." Proverbs 25:28. In other words, you are open to be attacked by any trespasser who comes against you, all because there is nothing protecting your being. Attack is fair game when your guards are not in place. When anything is free to come into your space, you welcome emotional and mental contamination.

If you ever wondered "when is it okay to trust," this is it. Trust comes in when boundaries are respected. Don't trust someone who has not proven themselves to be trustworthy. Trustworthiness has to be earned by observing your boundaries. Once your boundaries have been made clear and people choose to honor them, they have proven themselves to be trustworthy. If they violate a communicated boundary, it's time to forgive and let go.

A Broken Heart

We are sometimes prone to trust our hearts. This is mainly because that's what we are told to do. "Follow your heart." But, I'd like to challenge that. I don't think that it's good to trust what has the potential to cause ruin. "The heart is deceitfully wicked, above all things" (Jeremiah 17:9). The only way we can trust our hearts is if we have done our due diligence in guarding it. Some hearts have been lied to, broken, rejected and hurt; they are fearful, hopeless, suspicious, weary, malicious, worn out and calloused. They have been a revolving door, opening themselves to anything and anybody. They have been exposed to the worst of tragedies, traumatized and tormented. That's not your fault, but hurt is hurt. Hurt influences how we respond to people and situations. I would not trust this type of heart. Think about this: Hurt people, hurt people. In this case, hurt people will continue to hurt themselves by allowing their broken hearts to lead their lives. Would you trust me if I were unguarded and exposed to attack, vulnerable to hurt, full of rejection, fear and pain, having no motivation to seek healing? If your answer was a resounding NO, I get it. I would not trust my heart to lead either. The truth is we do this; we trust our hearts in anyone's hands because we think that it's a compass for our lives when really, "You have the power to tell your heart what to allow." ~Apostle Bryan Meadows.

A Healed Heart

Heart issues will not be resolved until they are acknowledged and dealt with. Only then can we allow God to reproduce wisdom and love, that we can then trust our hearts. Remember, we were created with all of this in tact, but due to the fall of Adam, we fell from this place of power. Now, we have been given the opportunity to regain power.

A guarded heart is more trustworthy. This is not to be confused with being so guarded that nothing can come in or go out. A guarded heart has allowed God to restore the broken pieces so that it can receive from a healthy place. This does not mean that hurt will never happen. It does mean that, with intention, healing will be sought after and boundaries will define relationships thereafter.

Just in case you were wondering, God does not pass out commands without providing His supernatural support. He wrote you a personal letter of support, hoping that you would embrace it. It says, "Dear friend, I hope all is well with you and that you are as healthy in body as you are strong in spirit" (3 John 1:2 NLT). The principle to take away is that guarding our hearts leads to a prosperous life. So, guess what? The way to guard your heart is to be careful of what you allow. You do this by having a boundary system.

Here are five boundaries of my own. I believe that every woman should have these.

"Sometimes it happens that a woman upon realizing how splendid she is in every way, goes about setting up her life so that it is just right in every way." ~Toni Rahman

1. I will not allow people to say or do hurtful things to me that I do not address appropriately at the proper time. When negative emotions are not acknowledged, you begin to harbor negative feelings for a person that could be avoided with a boundary.
2. I will not give a man my heart before I give him my boundaries. A man does not deserve me if he can't observe my boundaries. In keeping with that, I will not allow my romantic relationship to be reduced to text messages or any other form of digital communication. If he does not have time to call me, he does not want a relationship with me. I WILL NOT SETTLE!! Say that with me! I WILL NOT SETTLE
3. I will not shrink back to appease others. I will allow my light to shine, even in the midst of other women who have not yet discovered their lights. My light will help someone to find theirs.
4. I will not blame, shame or judge myself and others.
5. I increase the value of my time by avoiding all distractions and making the most of every minute. When I wake up in the morning,

before I acknowledge the agendas and expectations of family, friends and career, I acknowledge and spend time with the Holy Spirit to set my day in order and prepare myself for optimal performance.

Boundaries may actually seem completely selfish, but please accept this simple but profound truth once again! You can't help anyone else to breathe if you aren't breathing. So, put your breathing apparatus on first. You will be glad that you did. Between you and every person or situation lies the potential to make the best or worst of the relationship. Boundaries are truly beneficial in that they warrant the best. It's very important to know your limits, your breaking points, what you won't do and what you will stand up for.

TAKE RESPONSIBILITY. OWN IT!

"Implementing extreme ownership requires checking your ego and operating with a high degree of humility. Admitting mistakes, taking ownership and developing a plan to overcome challenges are integral to any successful team." ~Jocko Willink

Success did not leave you out. Though opportunities are not equally given, success is for those who want it bad enough and will maintain the discipline to achieve it. This may seem so simple and obvious, but it's worth saying over and over. YOUR COURSE IS UP TO YOU! It simply means that YOU determine your destiny, no matter what has happened to you and no matter what you have done. With the courage to take ownership, one is able to gain momentum and take command of one's life. This simple decision will cause very beneficial shifts.

More often than not, opportunities are left on the table because people wait for someone else to give it to them or validate their being able to get it. Some are also waiting on God to instruct them to do something that He has already given them authority and permission to do. Those days are over. We must abolish the mindset that things will be given to us with no pursuit or preparation. This may sound harsh, but it's really good news because you get to choose your life. No one gets to bar you from success or determine what your success looks like. You take responsibility by defining what success looks like for you.

Gone are the days where you sit, waiting for people to figure you out or beg you to tell them what's wrong. You must tell people your dreams, ideas, perspectives and needs. You might be talking to the person who can pray you into purpose, make a phone call or invest into your future. Don't make people guess. Doing so is taking a chance on your life, but with the opportunity to blame a situation for not getting what you really want from it. Humility and self-awareness are both shown through your ability to ask for what you need and want. This is how you become an influencer. Suddenly, people will want to know what you did and how.

Taking responsibility for your life translates into you attracting more opportunities. I think this is mainly because you are really creating your own opportunities and aligning yourself with purpose. When you have discovered purpose, you no longer beg and borrow. Sometimes, asking won't be necessary; opportunities will just come. The doors will open based on your preparation. I love this because no one will be able to say, "You have that opportunity because of me." Similarly, using someone else's name as an alibi for your mess-ups is over. You own it all, screw-ups and accomplishments.

Anyone who takes responsibility for their lives will address their failures, acknowledge their weaknesses, and build simultaneously. Every trial, whether self-inflicted or inflicted by others, becomes a stepping-stone leading to great possessions. Apparently, you are a conqueror because you are reading this book. Now, you have to go get what belongs to you. God does not allow a trial without filling it with rewards that you can take from it. Once you have taken your possessions, you become more than a conqueror. You are obligated to share your gains with the world.

Take responsibility for your life by using this framework from the word BREATHE

1. **Be** intentional. Because nothing just happens and you did not get this way overnight. So, guess what this means? Your best life is not going to fall into your lap, nor is it not going to change overnight. Be intentional about discovering the meaning of your life. We spend life becoming masters at everything except our own identities. The key to the life you want to live is inside of you. You won't find it comparing yourself to others. As a matter of fact, you have to eliminate people from this equation and get selfish about your quest to live your best life.
2. **Reprogram** your mindset. A mindset is the attitude of your overall thoughts. Your mindset is key in determining how you deal with any new adversity that comes your way. God will not pour out His favor on anyone who has a negative mindset. Reprogramming is going to start by believing the promises of God for your life and breaking every other agreement that is tied to dysfunction in your life. You are not less than, alone or missing anything. This mindset keeps you in a place of lack. Your God is the God of more than enough. Believe that your life is running over with an abundance of health, joy, love, peace, wealth, strength, competence and wisdom.
3. **Empower** yourself. This short but powerful mandate is expressive of the vigor with which you prepare for the road ahead. You will need spiritual, mental, and physical strength. God expects you to diligently gain strength and apply it in business and life. Self-empowerment is necessary to increase your capabilities.
4. **Accept** what has happened. Your destiny has to become more important than the tragedy. Acceptance will help you to change your perspective about what happened. "I am convinced that life is 10% what happens to me and 90% how I react to it. And so it is with you. We are in charge of our attitudes." ~Charles R. Swindoll

   As the co-creator of your life, you have the ability to

change any aspect of it once you have come to terms with it. You can't change what happened, but you can definitely make a decision to use what has happened to shape your future positively.

5. **Take** the limits off. Are you held back in life because of personal limitations or those you have placed on God? What keeps us stuck in lack is the way we define ourselves based on the opinions of others or our worst experiences in life. Unfortunately, we have been shaped by these toxic limits and stigmas. You have a God who can perform exceeding and above your requests, needs or desires and you can grow beyond your current capabilities. You can rise above the low-level opinion of who you are but, only if you believe that you can.
6. **Heal**. No matter what your situation looks like, you have a promise of healing. He is Jehovah Rapha. Healing sometimes comes through professional or spiritual counsel and it might start with mental and emotional healing. Seeking professional help does not diminish your value and your worth. It shows that you are mature enough to be honest about where you are. Your life is not without redemption. Your mental health is at risk more if you avoid the proper care.
   To heal you must forgive the situation and the individuals involved. Forgiving does not always mean reconciliation with the perpetrator, neither does it dismiss or minimize what happened.
7. **Expect** the best. God only wants the best for you. One of my favorite scriptures, Isaiah 30:18, says that God is earnestly waiting, expecting and looking to be good to you. Blessing you makes Him look good. So, don't allow anyone to make you feel guilty for expecting more favor, victory, love, prosperity or His companionship. God delights in your expectant hunger for Him and His blessings. You have more control of your future than your past. So, stay on the lookout for God's blessings.

Owning your mistakes provides the openness to correct, improve and move forward. I have made bad decisions, screwed over relationships and messed up opportunities. I created struggles for myself. I fought long and hard to justify my sin, just to feel like I was a good person. Once I found God's love, I was able to own my mistakes and love myself through the process of correction.

Life has its ways of trying to devalue us. Some misfortunes that you have experienced are not your fault. But, as your sister, I will not allow you to use it as an excuse to remain stagnant and allow the effects of trauma to prohibit you from charging forward in purpose. Your quality of life, even after a traumatic experience, is in your hands. Your development and growth are also in your hands. The enemy wants you to use your experiences as excuses to remain where you are. But, your Father is an expert at taking the biggest tragedy of your life and making it work for your benefit. The choice is yours. OWN IT!

Poor breathing affects our lives in various ways. Therefore, the principles for improving breathing habits should be aggressively pursued to yield desired results. Poor adherence to the previous breathing principles will reduce a person's ability to activate greatness, take hold of new opportunities, stay tough when life gets tough, defy the status quo and become a trailblazer. The problem will arise when our minds start insisting on returning to our former habits … habits that create complacent living. We will literally have to wean ourselves from toxic habits by taking every opportunity to breathe correctly. Without practicing proper breathing techniques, life will seem unproductive and draining. Over time, poor life skills will cause even more stress and less energy, but commitment to proven techniques will cause a whirlwind of change for the better.

CHAPTER 12

Breathe Again

This is what the Sovereign Lord says: "LOOK! I am going to put breath into you and make you live again! I will put flesh and muscles on you and cover you with skin. I will put breath into you and you will come to life."
Ezekiel 37:5 [NLT]

"Any quest for enhanced health and well-being should include improving your breathing habits as a basic component, since breathing is an integral part of us and is with us wherever we go. We have the opportunity to practice breathing exercises anywhere, at any time, in order to establish improved breathing habits simply, inexpensively, and effectively"~ Anders Olsson

What does breathing look like when it's done mindfully? Can both physical and psychological breathing be improved? How can I prevent choking? How is breathing related to thinking? Overall, successful breathing is accomplished the same way. Why does "breathe again" take on personal meaning? Why did this whole aspect of breathing catch me by surprise when I have been doing it my whole life? These are questions that I continue to ask myself. Indeed this subject of breathing has sparked a fire in my mind to continue learning and mastering the subject from every angle. Its scientific and spiritual purpose holds deep universal and personal principles that must be emphasized to empower humanity.

Breathlessness gives life no meaning and makes accomplishing anything a struggle. We become programmed to believe that our future will be a replay of the horrible things that happened in the past. Oddly, we do not consider our breathing as a tool to improve the quality of our lives. When breathing is not a priority, dreams, identity, energy, purpose, faith, love, esteem, courage, life, success, grit, hope, joy and peace are all compromised. We discussed in Chapter 1 that breathing can happen on its own. However, when breathing becomes an intentional focus, everything that is connected to the breath will improve.

Lack of proper breath or breathing incorrectly may have caused your life to bear the fruits of death. Another way to say it is psychological trauma has many effects on our lives. Some effects travel with us for many years after the experience. The traumatic experiences taint our beliefs, emotions, behaviors and definitely our thinking, sometimes, to the point that people develop physical ailments and mental health challenges. For such challenges, people really have to consider therapy in order to start the process of reclaiming their lives. The state that trauma leaves people in can be seen in the story of the valley of dry bones, described in Ezekiel 37:1-4. The bones, which represented people, were dry, dead, and brittle, without redemption and scattered from one end of the valley to the other. It's possible that in this vision, God was metaphorically showing Ezekiel a glimpse of dead people walking.

I know too well what this feels like. You know also or either you know people who are living, but their lives are mundane. Walking dead is a deep feeling of dread that leaves us with feelings of hopelessness and the inability to recover or regain control. Unfortunately, those traumatic moments create a setting in our minds and psychology that bar us from exploring what we could really make of our lives. The good news is at any point, no matter how bad breathing has become, your conscious attention to correcting it creates neural pathways leading to improvement. Can you believe that? No matter how agonizing you think your situation has become, you still have the power to change it. Start rewiring your brain to believe it by saying this. MY SITUATION IS CHANGING FOR THE BETTER. I HAVE THE POWER TO CHANGE ANY ASPECT OF MY LIFE.

The breathing techniques that you learned earlier can be applied to your daily life, but they may be hard to implement when old beliefs are still present. Distractions and external stimuli will always be loud, but your new truth will have to talk louder. Implementing these techniques will increase your ability to overcome stress with better breathing habits. So, to ensure we are breathing naturally, we have to commit our lives to the five breathing principles for better quality of life. In Chapter 1, I briefly mentioned how fitness trainers and instructors have connected to their purpose. They remind their clients to be well and give them the best advice for it. I mean, they are intrinsically linked. They know what to say and when to say it, normally, right in the nick of time. They thrive and get paid for giving us tips and information that will ultimately help us to be healthier and live longer.

"Inhale through your nose and exhale through your mouth," they tell us. "Inhale on the climb; exhale on the decline." The reminder to breathe is their way of saying, "Don't allow this challenge or this workout to stop you from doing what you know to do." In a sense, this book has given me the opportunity to be your trainer, as I have given you a personal call to action, sharing my perspectives and experiences with self-discovery, vision, systems, my boundary system, being REAL and how taking responsibility for your life is going to keep you alive. It's my way of reminding you to BREATHE. Inhale and exhale through your nose. TRY IT!

I N H A L E
E X H A L E

No! Don't just read the words. Really do it! I want you to immediately put this into action. It's time. Once you have read the next few lines of instruction, stop reading, close your eyes and concentrate on your breath. As you inhale through your nose, allow your stomach to fill with air. As you inhale, imagine a fresh wind of God's breath blowing in and around you. Let this wind bring healing from all sorrow and grief. Take a long exhale out of your mouth, allowing your stomach to deflate as you push the breath out. As you exhale, imagine that same fresh wind consuming and taking with it fear, rage, discouragement, lies, torment, stress, shame, disbelief, mediocrity, limitations and condemnation that have entered into your life through agreement, generational curses, and actions. Let this wind take everything that has come to wreak havoc in your life. Allow it to remove painful memories from traumatic experiences.

Ready. Set. Breathe.

Now, continue to breathe deeply as you read the next few pages. What you are doing naturally is resonating and confirming spiritual activity.

To this day, I am still baffled as to how easy it is to stop breathing when my body is exerting force. I had to go home and Google why such a spectacle is really even "a thing" anyway. The instinct to breathe is overpowered by the force that your body exerts while working out, but this only happens when no training has been done on how to develop the skill to do both simultaneously. What's really crazy is that most people don't know they are not breathing until they pass out or the trainer says, "Hey, don't forget to breathe." And they gasp! The same way it happens in the gym when you stop breathing while our body is exerting force, translates over into life. The pressure forces us to stop doing what should be done naturally and consistently, without thinking. You were created to naturally love, esteem, accept, forgive, challenge, invest in, embrace, believe in and set boundaries for yourself. But, it may seem like a struggle while simultaneously dealing with other pressures. Trauma, the identity thief, sometimes sends obstructions into our windpipes. We then start to choke, and this choking also causes panic. The pressure of it all breaks down the ability to foster self-care. Some actually begin to hate themselves, making it difficult or impossible to love anyone properly. This is the same concept on two different spectrums. What's true in the gym is still true for your soul. Breath is to the body what identity is to the soul. You must learn how to breathe and work to exert force at the same time. In the same way, we must learn to see ourselves as worthy after a mistake.

One who can't breathe also can't think, speak, dream, feel, live, love or respond. So, the lack thereof provides no sense of destiny or precision. It's the reason people waste time in toxic relationships. It's linked to low self-esteem and depression. It produces wicked leaders and immoral practices. It creates the billion-dollar stress industry. Breathlessness causes all of the frustration in the human race simply because people don't know they can change and be healed. They don't know that depression and anxiety are not hopeless situations. I've seen people get talked out of getting the help they need. I did that for a while and I had to learn the hard way that what I ignored would turn around and chase me. Your ability to breathe controls everything that you will ever do. Even, the wealthiest people of every culture and ethnic group are controlled by this phenomenon. Your ability to breathe should wake you up every morning with purpose and should help you sleep peacefully at night.

If we take a look at the story of Ezekiel, God's promise was to revive the bones back to life already, but God wanted to use Ezekiel as a mouthpiece to facilitate His plan. As the plot in Ezekiel 37 begins, God asks Ezekiel a question upon approaching a valley filled with bones. "Can these bones live?" God wanted to know if Ezekiel believed that the bones could be restored to their original place of dominating. God wanted to show Ezekiel that the life of those bones was in his faith and in his mouth. Ezekiel said, "God, I don't know how it can be done. Only you know."

I want to ask you the same question. Can your dry, dead bones live? Can your hope, dreams, competence, gifts, creativity, purpose, courage, fight, calling, anointing, ideas, love, uniqueness, confidence, love, peace, relationships, faith and your essence live again? Whether or not they live again is connected to your belief that they can live again and your willingness to speak life into them with faith. You have been given authority. Now, you must activate your belief to use it. What have you been saying to your situation before now? Your situation reflects your level of belief and what you have been confessing. Your words have created your world.

Does this sound like you? "I can't win for losing! If it's not one thing, it's another. Every time I take one step forward, I have to take ten steps backwards. I'm never going to win; bad things always happen to good people. I can't do that, I don't have the training! I'm too young, I'm too old, I don't have this, I don't have that, and I'm not qualified."

Or have you been saying, "I am unstoppable; my life is aligned with my purpose. Nothing and no one can hold me back. Today is the day that I will accomplish great exploits. I will never be broken again in my life! I am capable, I am resolute and ready to face all things. No weapon formed against me shall prosper. I will finish what I started?" The latter declarations are necessary. Your mindset must shift before your situation gets better. Even if your situation does not mirror what you are declaring, say it until you see it. And most of all BELIEVE it! Your declaration has spiritual implications that will change things in the natural.

To breathe AGAIN suggests that there was indeed a time that you were living and breathing. You were experiencing dominion like God designed. Maybe you were a business owner, had dreams of going to school or even starting a school. You were on the rise to your place of purpose, but something doused the flame of passion. Someone stole your dream or talked you out of it.

In Genesis 2:7, when God breathed His breath into Adam's nostrils, Adam became a living soul. Adam was just dirt and lifeless until God breathed His ruach breath (spirit) into him to create life. Ezekiel 37 parallels this first mention of God's breath. So, the same breath that created Adam in Genesis was used to put the dead bones back together again in Ezekiel 37. Breathing again will look different for everyone. For some, it's loving again; for others, it's giving yourself permission to prosper, and others may need to embrace the process, among hundreds of other meanings. Either way is regaining life and learning how to use better habits to keep yourself well. Intentional, conscious living is the overall goal. The benefits echo in the most important part of our being and is reflected in our day-to day-functions.

Breathing again is not always trying to create something from scratch, rather streamlining your focus to what God has already done and allowing it come to life. It involves using everything that God gave you and allowing it to create a cadence. It's allowing Him to use you as a conduit of revival. It's receiving His enabling power and not relegating grace to just its redemptive function. It's learning to breathe and endure pressure at the same time. It means being able to fight and build simultaneously, understanding that both are ongoing. It is allowing your light to shine on the outside so that your radiance will cause others to radiate. The truth is that you may have never known what God put on the inside of you. Either way, it's always been there. Just because you have not discovered your potential, your purpose or something about yourself does not mean that it's nonexistent. Similarly, just because others have not noticed your worth does not decrease your value. It means the search continues until you strike gold.

Remember, you are Righteous, Esteemed, Accepted and Loved (REAL). Believing this truth will repel every lie for you. This stamp of your identity does not change. It has been there waiting to be discovered, developed and activated. Your belief that you can change every aspect of your life will determine the next phase of your life. God changed things and created them by His words. You have the same power. It makes no difference where you have been. Knowing where you want to go, declaring it, and believing that you will get there is where you start.

How to breathe again?

INHALE

the fresh wind of God

EXHALE

Let the fresh wind take with it everything that has tried to hold you back.

INHALE

Realize Your Power

God has already equipped you to be who you need to be and accomplish what you need to accomplish. As His creation, you must consult Him to receive a full understanding of who and what that is. It may be hiding under agony, trauma, and adversity. The only way to understand purpose is to consult the creator of the purposed object. We all have a purpose. Everything that was made has a purpose and the lack of its fulfillment equals depression and deficient breath. Going to college does not equate to purpose. We were made for so much more than to go to college, incur debt, pay bills, get married, have children and die. Your real power comes in knowing that who you are called to be is greater than anything you can fathom. You need power! Part of your power is realizing where it comes from. Understanding the source of that power will allow it to be reproduced in your life. Jesus is the plug that connects us to our God and Father. By way of the complexity of your creation, there is no way for you to do anything without being connected to the Source. **Staying connected does not just improve life, it *IS* life.**

You have skills, talents, gifts and perspectives that are useless without the power that brings them to life. In order to keep growing, developing, producing and being successful, you must be connected. Unconnected computers are unproductive and will die. Connectivity is vital for your life and for those who you are meant to serve.

EXHALE

Understand Your Emotions

I am a person who does not like to pack. This is partly because I have not mastered the skill. I usually over pack until it's almost impossible to close the suitcase. Do you have that problem? The worst packing experience that I ever had was when I was in high school. I was heading to Savannah for the summer. While walking through the airport, the zipper on my suitcase split and my clothes started to fall out leaving a trail leading directly to me. Talk about embarrassing. I wanted to go back home and start the day all over. All of my business was exposed. Our emotions are set up the same way. When we just pack them down without giving them proper attention, they will spill over abruptly at the most inconvenient time. A perfect example is turning on the news and witnessing people going on shooting sprees in crowded buildings or when someone loses their job and goes back to mass murder the entire office. The same thing that happened to my suitcase happened in the perpetrator's emotions; they exploded at the seam. This is not something that just happens. Ignored and unacknowledged emotions were built up like pressure in a pipe and one slight movement caused the emotional pipe to burst.

The subject of emotions seems rudimentary and cliche, but is misunderstood and often disregarded. Proper knowledge will inform our human experience. An emotional state is determined by thoughts. So, if you notice a surge of negative emotions, one can only assume that the mindset, which is the collection of thoughts that preceded the emotions, was negative. Similarly, the way to create positive emotions is to eliminate negative thoughts and misconceptions. This will take consistency and focus. The problem is, some people have been talked into ignoring their emotions. When emotions are ignored, the opportunity to heal and gain control over them is forfeited.

Following an adverse life experience, adverse emotions form, but ignoring them is what worsens the emotional state, causing mental health problems. Having and maintaining healthy emotions is a key to achieving any type of success and helps when responding to new stressors.

Being clear about your emotional experiences and responding to them in a way that promotes resilience, regardless of what's going on externally, is good emotional health. For example, feeling low or sad does not always equal depression. To determine that you are depressed when you may not be can actually cause depression. You may simply be exasperated. Knowing that you are exasperated lessens the blow.

Emotional health is also associated with power. You were created to have power over your emotions, and not the other way around. But, having emotional intelligence comes from having a new and improved way of thinking. Being confidently vulnerable or being okay with being uneasy are two ways of embracing one's emotions. Once we become whole mentally, the rest of our lives will align. God gives us the power to be transformed by a renewed mind. That's why many problems are solved once an, "I am capable" mindset is achieved. Mental and emotional health are intrinsically linked for a reason. Breathing will start when you decide to become emotionally and mentally tough. So, the empowered life that you are made for requires you to continually renew your mind by aligning yourself strategically with God's lead. This is so that your life can manifest His promises. The meaningfulness of your calling is as essential as breathing, but there is no way to sustain everything that God can do in and through you without emotional stability and health. You must become a woman who knows how to navigate your emotions and allow them to inform you, rather than control you.

Nothing will put you in control of your life like combining the five principles for better breathing and watching the shift happen. These core fundamentals will give your life meaning and precision. If you're like me, you have many exploits to accomplish. So, you don't have time to remain asleep. Understand that people are conducting Google searches to find your solutions.

INHALE

Ask God for what you want.

EXHALE

He supplies needs and grants wants.

I have said a lot and it might seem complex, but here is what it boils down to.

Being able to breathe again is spiritual and has practical application, and you don't need anyone's permission to breathe, so stop looking for it! Deep down, we all know what we need to breathe again. Having the courage to expose it is another story. At some point or another, you might think, "I need to deepen my relationship with God," or "I need to stop seeking approval." You may also think, "I need to remove myself from toxic relationships" or "I should take better care of myself." These thoughts (or the like) are relaying the needs of your soul. You owe it to yourself to listen to them. It might be the hardest but the most beneficial decision that you have ever made because breathing again starts with self-examination. This is very uncomfortable because you have to look in the mirror and sometimes, you won't see what you are looking for. As a matter of fact, you might see the opposite, especially if you are looking for perfection. Stick with it! You might be worried about the struggle with self-acceptance, especially since you know your weaknesses, and you think people will find you out. UNDERSTAND THIS! God already knows the secrets that haunt you and He is not intimidated by them. You still have His nature and His image. You are still worthy of the love story that you often dream about, the prosperity that you have planned for and the supernatural insight of your Father. That case that you are building against yourself is holding you in contempt, and you might be missing out on the opportunity to bring your dreams to life.

INHALE

Your freedom is attached to your decision to commit.

EXHALE

God gives you the wisdom to decide solemnly.

Anyone who is breathing properly has reached a consistent cadence. Their breaths are like poetry. They have reached breath control and awareness, even with breathing being such an unconscious practice. They understand the power associated with every breath. Their successes outweigh their failures, and even their failures resemble success. Their breathing has a light, slow and shallow pattern and an excellent rhythm. People who have achieved this type of breathing make humble strides to the top, always staying mindful of their journeys and not allowing one win to mesmerize them. The confidence they exude is quiet. Nevertheless, when they talk about their success, it's to share with others and to create a path of succession for others who are not far behind. The need for validation has subsided. Guilt is demolished by their willingness to pay everything forward, which means no hoarding information. People who are breathing properly are making strides and have accepted God's grace, which allows them to not just be sustained but to be constantly developing and adding to their repertoire of wins. Notice that I never said that their lives are perfect. Even when a healthy pattern is reached, the human is still not without flaw.

On the other hand, people who are living with physical illnesses usually breathe more chaotically. This is because some illnesses stop the flow of oxygen to the brain. Anyone who is lacking oxygen can pass out due to unproductive breaths. This is where the importance of learning how to handle pressure and experience success at the same time comes in handy. Similarly, this is where knowing how to identify and tend to your emotions properly will become vital. Giving into the pressure of comparison and competition and the need for validation can cause the same breathless reaction in your emotional and mental space.

INHALE

You have the power.

EXHALE

You are connected to the Almighty God.

Your life's transformation did not just become complete when you accepted Christ into your life. You are continuously transforming and evolving. Some people will not like that. It will actually be a challenge for them to the point of feeling rejection on another level. Only now, you may be surprised as to your response in comparison with your response to rejection in the past. Breathing again may be less complex than you think.

There are several occasions in the Bible when people needed to be healed or delivered, or for the sake of my explanation, they needed to breathe again. God's response was not deep, mystical or super spiritual. He told a man that had been sitting by the pool for 38 years waiting to be healed to get up and take up his bed. He told the leprous man to go wash himself. He told Lazarus to come forth. These commands carried spiritual implication and results, but the application was very practical. In Isaiah 60, God commands, "ARISE and SHINE for your light has come and the glory of the Lord has risen upon you." I have learned to use the Word to guide my life and I love practical instructions like the ones that Jesus gives: go, get up, look, hear, ask, seek, knock, be and watch. My favorite is when He told Ezekiel, "Speak a prophetic message to these bones and say, 'Dry bones, listen to the word of the Lord! This is what the Sovereign Lord says: Look! I am going to put breath into you and make you live again! I will put flesh and muscles on you and cover you with skin. I will put breath into you and you will come to life.'" (Ezekiel 37:4-6) This entire book is dedicated to these verses of faith and instruction. Do you want to know what happened next? Of course, you do! You have to know what happened once he did what God said.

In the next part of the story, Ezekiel said, "So I spoke this message, just as he told me. Suddenly as I spoke, there was a rattling noise all across the valley. The bones of each body came together and attached themselves complete skeletons. Then as I watched, muscles and flesh formed over the bones. Then skin formed to cover their bodies, but they still had no breath in them."

Then God gave another instruction, "Speak a prophetic message to the winds, Ezekiel. Speak a prophetic message and say, 'This is what the Sovereign Lord says: Come, O breath, from the four winds! Breathe into these dead bones so they may live again.'

So I spoke the message as he commanded me, and breath came into their bodies. They all came to life and stood up on their feet-a great army" (Ezekiel 37:7-10).

You can literally command your life, body, mind, emotions to align with the Word of God. Whatever you speak to has to listen. Breathing Again is recovering ALL that you have lost and more, but it requires action and obedience. Just like you practice breathing physically, you will have to practice forgiving, accepting and loving yourself. You will have to practice dreaming again. As you work toward dreaming and accomplishing your dreams, becoming distracted can be easy, especially if you see others doing better. Give yourself permission to focus all of your energy on self-improvement so that you can reach the desired outcome. This is what I have noticed as I have implemented diaphragm exercises to strengthen my once weak diaphragm. I simply breathe into my diaphragm (the muscle that controls breathing), rather than my chest. As I inhale, I allow my breath to fill my stomach. I count to three on the inhale and four on the exhale. Doing so has improved my performance and endurance. I no longer hold my breath when I am training with high intensity. I can also talk longer and exercise with more force without becoming short of breath and feeling like

I need a break within the first couple of minutes. This is a testament to the fact that sometimes, the smallest adjustments yield the most beneficial changes. Whether your journey is spiritual, physical, mental, emotional or a combination of them all, it is better for you to create goals for your journey and enjoy reaching them. Remember to show grace if you fall back, just don't turn back. Reset and keep moving forward.

If you continue to read the story of the dry bones, you will find that, not only did they stand up, they were reunited and realigned with the original plans of God and returned to their promised land. This was the land of abundance and overflow … a land that provided them with everything they needed. They received God's love and His grace—a love that never fails. The same love that is reckless to the point of being jealous for you violently consumes everything in its path for you. I love the lyrics to the song Reckless, which says, "Oh, the overwhelming, never-ending reckless love of God. It chases me down, fights til I'm found, leaves the 99. I couldn't earn it and I don't deserve it, still you give yourself away." IT'S TRUTH! His love for you would still kick down mountains, even if you never walked through another church door.

If you have character issues that you are not proud of, give them to God. He will not turn you away. This gives God the room to do His best work on you. You don't have to try to be something you're not. Tell the Lord what you are trying to accomplish and He will breathe a fresh wind of enabling power to help you accomplish the task.

Can I tell you something? As if this conversation just started…

Daughter, the Lord is extending a great invitation for you to be a part of something extraordinary and to be that change this world needs. This is so you can impact generations unborn. Your restoration, renewal and resurgence has to be something that you are committed to faithfully. You can't keep putting your dreams and your life on hold. Someone's life is depending on you getting yours together. This is because God has already chosen you for this work, which means He has already approved what you have on hold. He has created you to be confrontational in order to liberate those who have been oppressed. You may have been told that God does not need you, but I beg to differ. He does. He can always find someone else, but He has chosen YOU! He wants to use the leadership abilities that you have innately. He needs you to go into the trenches to snatch those who have fallen. He needs your voice for those who have no voice to echo to nations and to begin movements that empower women and men to fulfill their purposes. God needs your bold personality and for you to be unapologetic in your calling. He needs your fervent prayer life to bring Heaven to Earth. He needs your uncanny knack to captivate the hearts of the lost and call people to action. He needs your strength in collecting information to teach, because you can relate to others and dig into their feelings. He knows that you will understand what they don't say. He needs you to affirm His heart to those who are condemned. He needs your knack to take people from ignorance to competence. He needs YOU. Not only does God need you, but we need you. Only first, you have to make sure you are breathing. Your first and highest calling is to love yourself (after God, of course). If you have ever felt hopeless or thought that your life was beyond redemption, THINK AGAIN. If you have ever doubted that there is a purpose for your birth, THINK AGAIN. Maybe your life is a replica of mine. The Adverse Childhood Experience Study (ACES) shows that children who had an incarcerated parent, experienced rape or molestation, and many other hallmarks of an agonizing childhood are more likely to experience health problems. However, by way of our spiritual birthright and physical capability, we have the power to change our outcome. It does not matter where you are, you have the opportunity, even in the face of a crisis, to recover everything that was lost. All of creation is waiting on you to know who you are so you can use that knowledge and take your rightful position in this world. It's time to take ownership of your life so that you can help others find theirs. Thankfully, we are all given the opportunity to renew our minds daily. Daughter, God wants you to know that He will not allow you to be deceived. This is why He sent an Angel to help you breathe. LET'S BREATHE!

INHALE
Receive God's grace to function at your highest.
EXHALE
Release everything that was holding you captive to mediocrity.
INHALE
Allow God's dreams to become your dreams.
EXHALE
Release the opinions of others that held your dreams captive.
INHALE
Your needs are worth being met.
EXHALE
No more begging.
INHALE
Laugh.
EXHALE
Cry if you need to.
INHALE
Take what belongs to you.
EXHALE
Have the courage to release what does not belong to you.
INHALE
Don't just say I can.
EXHALE
Say I WILL.
INHALE
Get the help you need, even if it means seeing a Psychiatrist.
EXHALE
Ask God to lead you to the doctor who is assigned to your situation.
INHALE
Go after your purpose.
EXHALE
DUMP the need for validation.
INHALE

Stop trying to deserve God's love and acceptance.
EXHALE
God's love for you predates your existence.
INHALE
The Spirit of God created you and the breath of the Almighty revives you (Job 33:4).
INHALE
You are capable.
EXHALE
You are connected to God.
INHALE
You are the daughter of a King.
EXHALE
All of your needs are met from His riches.
INHALE
Speak to your situation.
EXHALE
Your brain responds to your command.
INHALE
Love yourself.
EXHALE
Detox from every lie that held you back.
INHALE
Reconnect with Jesus. He is the plug.
EXHALE
Regain your personal power.
INHALE
Understand that your affliction served a purpose.
EXHALE
Think again.
INHALE
Let your light shine.
EXHALE
Focus on YOU for a change.
INHALE
Don't shrink back.
EXHALE

No more fear.
INHALE
Be bold.
EXHALE
Release doubt.
INHALE
Accept your strengths and weaknesses.
EXHALE
You are not disqualified.
INHALE
See yourself the way God sees you.
EXHALE
You get another chance.
INHALE
God sees you and hears you.~ El ROI
EXHALE
Failures do not determine identity or the future.
INHALE
You can admit your limitations.
EXHALE
Perfection is not REAL.
INHALE
God is fighting for you.
EXHALE
Your success is God's greatest wish.
INHALE
You will not die, but LIVE.
EXHALE
You win.
INHALE
Dream again.
EXHALE
Ask again.
INHALE
Live again.
EXHALE
Look again.

INHALE
Love again.
EXHALE
Hope again.
INHALE
Apply again.
EXHALE
Pray again.
INHALE
Smile again.
EXHALE
Cry again.
INHALE
You are fearfully and wonderfully made.
EXHALE
You have substance, even though you're imperfect.
INHALE
God's thoughts of you are precious; they outnumber the grains of sand on any beach.
EXHALE
Your enemies are God's enemies.
INHALE
God knows your anxious thoughts.
EXHALE
God knows you inside and out.
INHALE
Forgive again.
EXHALE
Go again.
INHALE
Move again.
EXHALE
Expect again.
INHALE
Own your mistakes.
EXHALE
Love yourself through the development process.

INHALE
Give yourself permission without feeling like you need it from others.
EXHALE
The wait is over

BREATHE AGAIN PRAYER

God, I come before you in the mighty name of Jesus. I thank you for even allowing me to approach your throne boldly to find grace and ask for help in my time of need. I thank you for the opportunity to be exactly who you created me to be, despite what has happened in my past. Thank you for walking with me during the season of my life that I rejected you and the times when I only came to you when I needed something. Supernatural God, the Creator of all, thank you for the dawning of each new day and each new season as it represents a time for change and new beginnings I am grateful. You fill each day with infinite possibilities and new discoveries. Now that I have taken the first steps towards the best part of my life, I want to be led by you. In the past, I tried to go my own way, and that did not work. So, I surrender all of my ways to your perfect will. Open my eyes to see the strategies that will help me perform at my best. The times that I have come up short, you have been the filler. When I was broken, you mended me and when I needed peace, you showed up as the Prince of Peace. I give you everything that I have and all that is within me, including my heart, my mind, my body and my life. God take each part of me and purify it. Lord, I ask that you would take out all of the stress, fear, torment, grief, shame, pain and infirmity that has taken up residence. Remove it from every fiber of my being. I claim the stress-free and abundant life you died for me to have. Heavenly Father, I ask that you would send the blood of Jesus to the deepest places that no one can see and heal unresolved and unidentified pain. Holy Spirit, I welcome you to take full control of my life. I GIVE UP! Not on life, but on trying to please anyone other than you. I give up on allowing everyone to use me, but you. Lord, you are my Father and my Savior, and I ask boldly for you to get the glory out of my life. Cause my life to be in strategic alignment with your plans and purpose. Contend with anything that even tries to touch my life. Let me discern by your Spirit any cruel or impure motives of others. You have set before me life and death, and I thank you for giving me the mind to choose properly. I declare before Heaven and hell that I chose life and peace, health and joy. I chose to praise you. I choose to embrace your love. You make me to know that I am nothing without you. I hardly do everything right, but I'm desperate for you. God, dispatch your angels that are assigned to my life to shield and protect me from evil. Keep me from fear, manipulation, untimely death, dream snatchers and all darkness. Now that I know that I am the light of the world, I will use my light to engulf the hearts of others and I will make your name great. God, your grace is perfect; it is more than anything that I could ever ask for. Sometimes, I wonder why I didn't know about it sooner. I also wonder why you chose me. Even now, I am grateful and I will share the message of your grace with everyone I come in contact with, even those who've hurt me because they need it the most. Like Ezekiel, I now command every dead thing in my life that should be alive to hear the Word of the Lord and live. God, I create the space for you to continuously be a source of new life as I breathe again. AMEN.

SOURCES

How to raise your self esteem, Branden, Nathaniel, 1987
Page 5

Success Habits, Brendon Burchard

The Journey, Bryan Meadows

Helmstetter, Shad, PH.D., The Power of Neuro-plasticity

Dr. Caroline Leaf show. Episode 6 season 4

The Demon Dictionary: Kim Daniels page 8-9

Source: Reported in Tony Campolo, It's Friday but Sunday's Comin. (Word, 1985)

Start with Why Simon Sinek

John Maxwell, Thinking for a Change, 2003 page 78-79

Wilkinson, Bruce, Talk Thru the Bible

Motherrisingbirth.com chapter 1.

http://www.normalbreathing.com/Articles-breathing-maximum-brain-oxygenation.php

Anders Olsson, The Power of Your Breath,

www.proflowers.com article name: How flowers get their colors,

Joyce Meyer bible
Commentary
Strong's concordance 7307

Ramsay, William M. "Galatia," *International Standard Bible Encyclopedia.* Edited by James Orr. Blue Letter Bible. 1913. 5 May 2003

https://www.blueletterbible.org/study/misc/name_god.cfm.

https://storiesforpreaching.com/youre-the-son-of-God/

reported in Tony Campolo, It's Friday but Sunday's Comin. (Word, 1985)

http://www.myredeemerlives.com/namesofgod/adonai-elohim.html

http://study.com/academy/lesson/omnipotent-omniscient-and-omnipresent-god-definition-lesson-quiz.html

www.independent.co.uk/life-style/quarter-life-crises-age-most-likely-job-work-relationships-link

American-historama.org

www.news4jax.com/news/local/jackdsonville/man-with-no-name-finally-knows-real-identity

http://www.biblebb.com/files/KSS/kss-bleedingwoman.htm

Mark 5:24-34

Stay connected

What does breathe again mean to you? Answer on social media and use the hashtag #breatheagain

www.angelpdevone.com
IG @angelpdevone
Periscope @angelpdevone
FB Angel P Devone
info@angelpdevone.com

Made in the USA
Columbia, SC
11 June 2019